RAIN

A Play in Three Acts

Founded on W. SOMERSET MAUGHAM'S *Story*
" *Miss Thompson.*"

by

JOHN COLTON and
CLEMENCE RANDOLPH

SAMUEL FRENCH

LONDON
NEW YORK TORONTO SYDNEY HOLLYWOOD

COPYRIGHT 1923 BY LIVERIGHT INC.
COPYRIGHT (ACTING EDITION) 1948 BY SAMUEL FRENCH LTD

ISBN 0 573 01368 3

RAIN

Produced at the Garrick Theatre, London, on 12th May, 1925, with the following cast of characters :—

In the order of their appearance

MRS. HORN, AMELÍA	*Barbara Gott*
CORPORAL HODGSON	*John Rockey*
PRIVATE GRIGGS	*James Dyrenforth*
SERGEANT O'HARA	*Stuart Sage*
JOE HORN, the Trader of Pago Pago . .	*Shep Camp*
MRS. DAVIDSON	*Marda Vanne*
DR. MACPHAIL	*J. H. Roberts*
MRS. MACPHAIL	*Hilda Bruce-Potter*
SADIE THOMPSON	*Olga Lindo*
QUARTERMASTER BATES, of the " Orduna " .	*Gilbert Ritchie*
REV. ALFRED DAVIDSON	*Malcolm Keen*

Natives ; a Girl, a Boy, an Old Man, an Old Woman, a Policeman.

The action of the play takes place in the living room of Joe Horn's hotel-store on the Island of Pago Pago in the South Seas, during the rainy season. The time is the present.

———

SYNOPSIS OF SCENES

ACT I.   Early morning.
ACT II.   Two days later. Late afternoon.
ACT III. SCENE 1. Four days later. Night.
　　　　　SCENE 2. Early the following morning.

RAIN

ACT I

The SCENE *of the play is the public living room of* JOE HORN'S *Hotel-Store on the Island of Pago Pago in the South Seas.*

It is to be presumed that the hotel-store is a frame building of two storeys, with broad verandahs on both floors. It stands on a little incline, a short distance from the wharf at which steamers touch. Apart from the government buildings and a small U.S. Naval Station, it is the only occidental habitation in this tiny island.

The audience views the room from a slight angle, enabling them to see the verandah, which extends across the stage at R. The verandah is railed in iron-work painted yellow, supported by wooden pillars upholding a roof of corrugated iron.

(*See the* GROUND PLAN *at the end of the play.*)

The floor of the room is covered with greasy matting, and the walls are papered only in vague patches with paper that at one time or another had gold markings on it. Where the paper has peeled, crumbling plaster and white-washed laths show through. From the ceiling, at C., hangs a lamp worked by chains. The lamp is framed in a tin and glass arrangement, and when lit casts on the floor an oval pool of reddish-gold light.

The centre of the back wall is broken by a rickety staircase, projecting out into the room. The stairs reach a half landing on stage, then turn and lead to a higher landing off-stage to R.

Upstage in the L. wall are swing doors. By the sign over them we learn that they lead into the general store of Pago Pago, of which Joe Horn is the proprietor. Downstage in the L. wall is another door, recessed, and covered by a bedraggled Japanese bead curtain, stringy, bitten, and very old. This leads into the room which Sadie Thompson occupies later.

On the walls are lithographs and other objects, as described in the furniture plot.

In the R. upstage corner is a shabby sofa upholstered in maroon plush. Near it, an ornate oak table, on which is a fat German lamp with a shade on which poppies have been painted.

At L.C., somewhat downstage, is a narrow dining table with a shabby red cloth. It is littered with dreary castors, salt cellars and sugar bowls, protected from insects by swathings of mosquito netting. Five iron café chairs, painted green, are set at this table.

At R.C. is a dilapidated rattan deck-chair in which JOE HORN habitually reclines. By it is a stool or coffee table, on which are a box with a few cigars, and a battered volume of Nietzche.

There is an upright rattan chair below and R. *of Horn's chair, and another down* R., *and by this a small café table.*

There is a long step to the verandah, extending almost the entire length of the entrance. Below the downstage end of the step is a hat rack and a receptacle containing a large and battered umbrella for the use of visitors. On the verandah are two rattan or painted iron chairs, set near the rail.

Beyond the verandah we see a vista of sky, sea, beach and distant mountains. Nearby, bright green palm trees lift their branches, and brilliant flowers in riotous confusion.

When the CURTAIN *rises, the scene is bathed in the intense sunlight of early morning. Insects buzz and birds sing. In the distance we hear the low chanting of natives at work, broken once or twice by the booming blast of a steamer's siren.*

Then a native girl enters from down R., *on the verandah. She wears the* lava lava, *the native costume of the South Seas, and carries on her head a basket of pineapples. She crosses indolently and gracefully to* L., *and enters the store. She is followed by a native boy, and an old man, also wearing the* lava lava. *The boy carries fruit and the old man a basket of toys and ferocious masks of Kanaka workmanship. They are all chattering and laughing good-humouredly. After them comes an old woman, chewing betel-nut and balancing on her back a pole to which are attached fish bladders and pieces of dried shark.*

They all enter the store and chatter is heard within. The ship's siren is heard again. The natives emerge from the store, cross to the verandah and sit about; some of them begin to make wreaths from a basket of flowers. As the action of the play proceeds, they disappear aimlessly and unobtrusively. From afar comes the plaintive wail of a native flute and the low strumming of a stringed instrument.

As the natives reach the verandah, there enters from the store AMEENA, *who is* MRS. JOE HORN. *She is a large and darksome lady, the colour of deep* café au lait, *and ten years ago she was very pretty. Now she is enormously fat and oozes rather than walks. Her bare feet are thrust into carpet slippers and her oily black hair is skewered into a wizened knot at the back of her head. She crosses to the verandah and looks off, shading her eyes from the too bright sun. The siren is heard again and she turns, and waddles back towards the store.*

She opens the door and calls shrilly :

MRS. HORN. Joe ! Joe ! Why-for you ain't up, hein ? The boat comes already to the jett-ee . . . get yourself dressed.

(*She returns to the table, surveys it, fanning herself. She then moves away to* L.C. *At this moment two Marines enter via the verandah. They are* PRIVATE GRIGGS *and* CORPORAL HODGSON, U.S.M.C. *Both are clean-cut, fresh-skinned, good-humoured young lads, dressed in the bleached khaki uniforms of the Tropics.*)

HODGSON.   Hullo ! Tell us, Mamma—Where's you old man ?
MRS. HORN (*with scorn; coming to* R. *of the table*). My old man ?
Hui He ! (*She gestures with her shoulders, expressing helplessness.*)
GRIGGS (*moving in with* HODGSON). Lay off the moans, old lady—
cheer up ! (*He slaps her back and she begins to smile broadly.*)
Much better—much better—she's real fascinating when she smiles,
ain't she, Bill ?
HODGSON (R. *of the deckchair; winking at* GRIGGS). Garod, what
a valentine !
MRS. HORN (*regaining her good humour*). Get along, you scamps
—what you want—hein ?
GRIGGS.   Bring out a white man's cigarette for the love of God !
MRS. HORN (*with an empty gesture*). Cigarettes ! Not got yet.
HODGSON (*astonished*). Not got yet ! The boat's in, ain't it ?
Jack here and I are 'bout ready to commit murder for a Lucky.
MRS. HORN.   The boat is in. Yes . . . (*Points to the store.*) But
what does he care—that man—my husband ? He sleeps.
GRIGGS.   I tell you, mamma, if we don't get a human smoke
pretty soon we'll get fierce. Where is he ?

(MRS. HORN *gestures in the direction of the store, folds her hands,
          closes her eyes and gives a snore.*)

GRIGGS.   Asleep, huh ? Just wait—(*He starts for the store.*)
HODGSON.   We'll have that bird on his feet and down to the
dock—chop-chop pronto ! (*He crosses* L., *after* GRIGGS.)
MRS. HORN (*jeeringly*). I think so—no !
HODGSON (*at the door*). I think so, yes.

(*They clatter into the store noisily.* MRS. HORN *laughs and sits*
                    R. *of the table.*)

(SERGEANT TIM O'HARA *enters,* R. *He is a tall, well set-up fellow
of about thirty-five—stalwart, tanned, pleasing to look at. He is
fair with kindly blue eyes and jolly smile, and very spick and span
in his morning whites.*)

MRS. HORN.   Hello—there, you O'Hara—
O'HARA.   —Morning, mamma. (*Moving in, to* R.C.) How is it
by you today ?
MRS. HORN (*sniffing*). Not so good.
O'HARA.   Not so bad, I guess—
MRS. HORN.   Mebbe a bit good. Plenty bad.
O'HARA (*crossing below* MRS. HORN, *to* L.C.). What's the trouble?
—Old man acting up again ?
MRS. HORN (*indignantly, rising*). How you talk—What you say—
my husband is very, very good man—sleep too much—mebbe—
drink—sometimes a little mebbe too, sometimes not come home—
mebbe no—but always he is very, very good man, my husband—

(O'HARA *laughs.* GRIGGS *and* HODGSON *enter, lugging with them*
JOE HORN, *the trader of Pago Pago.* HORN *is a monstrously large*

*man.   He has tousled white hair and a broad, good humoured,
shrewdly tolerant countenance.   He stands rubbing his eyes—a
somewhat ludicrous figure in dirty white dungaree trousers and
pyjama coat.   His bare feet are thrust into broken down, laceless
shoes.*)

HORN.   Not so fast—not so fast—what's all this ?   Where am I ?
MRS. HORN.   Where is he—he asks.   (*She turns up, above the
table.*)
HORN (*smiling and rubbing his eyes*).   To be sure—as usual we
find ourselves at home.   Bosom of the family.   Greetings, fair one,
greetings.
MRS. HORN (*sniffing*).   Greetings.   He gives his wife greetings !
HORN (*to* O'HARA, *moving to below the table*).   Naturally I greet
my blossom of delight—Damn fine woman, Mrs. Horn.   Excellent
woman.   Sometimes I wish she was in Hell.
MRS. HORN.   Always he jokes like that.   My Joe—Such a man
he is for fun !
HORN (*agreeably*).   Well, what are we waiting for ?   (*Crossing to
R.C.*)   Why this tension ?   What's expected of me ?
O'HARA.   The *Orduna's* in, Joe—been in for an hour.
HORN.   What of it ?   (*He sits in the deckchair.*)
MRS. HORN (*screamingly, moving down* R. *of the table*).   What of
it !   What of it—the store is empty, no calico, no sardines, no
peaches, no corned beef !   No nothing !

(GRIGG *and* HODGSON *have moved* R., *to above the deck-chair.*)

HORN (*lazily*).   Old Mother Hubbard—
GRIGGS (R. *of the chair, hoisting* HORN *to his feet*).   On your feet,
mate, we want cigarettes !
HORN (*sitting again and lighting a cigarette calmly*).   Go away !
It is much too early in the morning for life's burdens—let me first
accustom myself to the fact that another day has come to join
eternity—besides, this is Sunday, is it not—six days shalt thou
labour—
GRIGGS.   Bush-wa !—You should talk of Sunday.

(*He and* HODGSON, *who is* L. *of the chair, propel* HORN *out of it.*)

HORN (*wearily*).   If I must—I must.   (*He chucks* MRS. HORN
under the chin, then pauses in ponderous mischief.)   Wait a minute !
Did you boys ever hear of Dr. Johnson ?
GRIGGS.   Sure !   He was surgeon on the *Utah*.
HORN (*scornfully*).   No, my boy, no !   Dr. Samuel Johnson !
HODGSON (*wearily*).   Well, what did he do, Joe ?

(HORN, HODGSON *and* GRIGGS *start for the verandah,* HORN *in the
lead.*   HORN *suddenly stops again and turns towards* HODGSON
and GRIGGS.)

HORN (*beginning to pontificate*). Great works, says Dr. Johnson are not performed by strength alone, but by perseverance—

GRIGGS (*urging him to keep moving*). Yeah, that's right, Joe.

HORN (*deliberately walking as slowly as possible towards the verandah*). He who walks three hours a day will in seven years circle the globe.

(GRIGGS *and* HODGSON *propel* HORN *with difficulty out of the scene. They disappear beyond the verandah.*)

O'HARA (*reflectively; sitting on the edge of the table*). Nothing like few wants and thorough satisfaction with what one's got, and every man is his own king.

MRS. HORN (*nodding amiably, following the others off with her eyes*). King ! Sure, my father one time King Pago Pago here. I princess. I marry Joe Horn, Christian way, now Joe all same King. Alu he ca mi kapi.

O'HARA (*rising and strolling toward the verandah*). You gonna tell me all that again ? I've heard it a million times !

MRS. HORN (*tartly*). What you know ? You only sailor man. Hui !

O'HARA (*leaning on the verandah rail, looking off down* R.). Here's some people coming mamma, off the *Orduna*.

MRS. HORN (*waddling toward him*). Pipple come—pipple come here ?

O'HARA. Yeah—look like missionaries.

MRS. HORN. Mee-sion-arry ? (*Turning and hurrying* L.) God dam ! I run !

(*She exits into the store.*)

O'HARA. Me too.

(*He hastens after her.*)

(*A moment later* MRS. DAVIDSON *enters, followed by* DR. *and* MRS. MACPHAIL. MRS. DAVIDSON *is a little woman with dull brown hair, stiffly arranged. Her face is long, like a sheep's, but she gives no impression of foolishness, rather of extreme alertness—she has the quick movement of a bird. She is dressed in black china silk and wears around her neck a gold chain from which dangles a small cross. Her prominent blue eyes look forth sharply from behind gold-rimmed pince-nez. Her voice is high, metallic and without inflection. It falls on the ears with a hard monotony, irritating to the nerves, like the clamour of a pneumatic drill.*)

MRS. DAVIDSON. This is the trader's place, I believe.

(*She gestures to* DR. *and* MRS. MACPHAIL, *who have lingered on the verandah observing the landscape. They enter.* DR. MACPHAIL *is a man of forty, thin, pinched, with a bald patch on his crown. He is a man of humour and reticence. One likes him instinctively. MRS. MACPHAIL is a woman a little younger than her husband.*)

She is the indefinite type of person, who looks like everyone else—
polite, acquiescent, rather sweet and not at all sure of herself.)

DR. MACPHAIL (*to his wife; on her* R.). Now don't worry about
the baggage, my dear. It will be taken care of in plenty of time.
(*Seeing sign, he reads:*) " Pago Pago General Store, Joe Horn,
Prop."

MRS. MACPHAIL (*looking about curiously*). No one seems to be
about ! (*Moving into the room.*) I do hope we can get some lunch
here, Robert. We breakfasted so early I feel rather faint.

MRS. DAVIDSON. The trader's wife serves meals here I believe—
they're very bad I'm told, but we can't expect very much from Pago
Pago. Thank heaven we shan't be here for long.

DR. MACPHAIL (*crossing up* L.). Well, anyway I'll see what I can
do.

(*He exits into the store.*)

MRS. MACPHAIL (*to* MRS. DAVIDSON). Is this a hotel ?

MRS. DAVIDSON. Well, not exactly. (*She sits* R. *of the table.*)
This man Horn accommodates people from time to time while
they're changing boats, that's all, I believe.

MRS. MACPHAIL. Oh, you've been here before, then ?

MRS. DAVIDSON. Oh yes, Mr. Davidson and I were here on
our way to America a year ago.

MRS. MACPHAIL (*moving to the upstage end of the verandah,
looking off*). How beautiful it all is. I hope we'll have time for
a walk, after lunch.

MRS. DAVIDSON (*rising and moving up* R.). Oh, there's nothing to
see but a few native huts and the Naval Station and the Governor's
house. (*She points.*) That's it. Just around the corner.

MRS. MACPHAIL (*astonished*). Is *that* the Governor's house ?
Why, it's only a bungalow.

MRS. DAVIDSON (*turning back into the room*). As I say, there's
nothing to see, but when my husband comes back we'll take a turn
about—it can't take him long to transfer our baggage.

(MRS. MACPHAIL *moves down and they both seat themselves at the
dining-room table.*)

MRS. MACPHAIL (*seated* R. *of the table*). I must confess I rather
dread the rest of the trip on the schooner.

MRS. DAVIDSON (*seated above the table*). You well may ! But
think of Mr. Davidson and myself ! We shall have ten days more
on the schooner when we leave you at Apia. (*She pauses then remarks
sharply.*) I'm sorry, though, you're getting your first impressions
of the South Seas from these Islands.

MRS. MACPHAIL (*innocently*). Why ?

MRS. DAVIDSON (*as though imparting a dreadful fact*). They're
far below the moral standard—the steamers touching here make
the people unsettled. Then there's the Naval Station—that's bad

for the natives. (*Shaking her head at the awful thought.*) Oh ! It's almost a hopeless task for the missionaries here.

MRS. MACPHAIL (*curiously*). Really !

MRS. DAVIDSON (*very earnestly*). Your husband's coming is most timely, Mrs. MacPhail ! Mr. Davidson was saying only last night that at last the Institute had sent the right man for the right job. Diseased conditions here are terrific !

MRS. MACPHAIL (*as though to change the subject*). I suppose we'll be stationed several months in Apia. What's it like there ?

MRS. DAVIDSON (*determined the subject shall continue*). It's a dreadful place ! The missionaries haven't as much power as they ought to have, and the place is over-run with American prostitutes.

MRS. MACPHAIL (*taken aback*). How horrible !

MRS. DAVIDSON (*drawing her chair closer to* MRS. MACPHAIL *and speaking almost in a whisper*). You remember what we were talking about the other night ?—Have you told Dr. MacPhail yet ?

MRS. MACPHAIL (*hesitatingly*). You mean about what their marriage customs used to be ?—Yes !

MRS. DAVIDSON (*with relish*). What did he say ?

MRS. MACPHAIL (*slowly*). Well—he never says very much, but I'm sure he thought it was perfectly awful.

MRS. DAVIDSON (*eagerly continuing*). You made it all clear to him I hope ? About what the old men and women used to do—about the common house—about the festivals ?

MRS. MACPHAIL (*rather flustered*). I—tried—to—

(*Her speech is broken by* DR. MACPHAIL, *who enters from the store, followed by* MRS. HORN.)

DR. MACPHAIL (L. *of the table, to his wife and* MRS. DAVIDSON). This is our hostess, Mrs. Horn—she has promised us some lunch. (*To* MRS. HORN.) About twelve you said, didn't you ?

MRS. HORN (*languidly; above the* L. *end of the table*). Oh, a long time. I go send girl now—kill chicken—come home by'n-by.

(*She crosses,* R., *and exits.*)

DR. MACPHAIL. H-m ! Colourful, if not aesthetic !

MRS. DAVIDSON (*to* DR. MACPHAIL). Well ? I hear that Mrs. MacPhail has been telling you some of the things about these islands which I couldn't, even though you are a doctor.

DR. MACPHAIL (*mildly interested*). What things ?

MRS. DAVIDSON (*warming to her subject*). About the moon dancing, the sugarcane festival, etcetera !

DR. MACPHAIL (*rather amused*). Ah, yes, yes...

MRS. DAVIDSON. Can you imagine such depravity ! Such dances !

DR. MACPHAIL (*whimsically, as he strolls to the deck-chair*). Tell me Mrs. Davidson, when you were a little girl did you ever dance around the Maypole ?

MRS. DAVIDSON (*mystified*). It's quite possible that I did. Why ?

DR. MACPHAIL (*turning to her, enjoying himself immensely*). Oh nothing, except that I believe the custom of the Maypole had its origin in festivals somewhat similar to those you have been telling my wife about.

MRS. DAVIDSON (*totally lost as to what it's all about*). I haven't the slightest idea what you're talking about.

DR. MACPHAIL (*sitting in the deck-chair; with satisfaction*). Yes, that's possible.

(SERGEANT O'HARA *makes his appearance, urging before him two natives who seem determined to take their own good time.*)

O'HARA. You boys hurry up. Go down dock running. Many fella want cigarettes. Hurry up ! Plenty rain soon coming.

(*He exits.*)

MRS. MACPHAIL (*rising, and moving to the verandah*). It can't be going to rain, can it ?

MRS. DAVIDSON (*rising, and joining her*). Very likely. This is the beginning of the rainy season.

MRS. MACPHAIL (*on the verandah step, upstage end*). But the sky is so blue !

MRS. DAVIDSON (*pointing toward the sky*). Do you see those fleecy little grey clouds ? The shape of spoons—they look like puffs of smoke.

MRS. MACPHAIL (*looking as directed*). Yes.

MRS. DAVIDSON. Note how they are gathering together. We shall certainly have rain in a little while.

(SERGEANT O'HARA *re-enters down* R., *on the verandah.*)

O'HARA (*calling off to the natives*). Hurry up, now ! Go beach runnun ! Make bring damn double quick ! (*He turns to enter.*)

MRS. DAVIDSON (*to* O'HARA). Young man, do you know whether our baggage has been taken from the ship ?

O'HARA (*touching his hat*). No ma'am. I don't know a thing about it.

MRS. DAVIDSON (*exasperated*). Oh ! the procrastinations of these people are terrible ! (*She moves back into the room.*)

O'HARA (*ironically*). Yes ma'am, they are terrible. (*Turning to the verandah.*) Terrible indeed ! (*He lounges against the verandah rail.*)

(MRS. DAVIDSON *sits* R. *of the table.* MRS. MACPHAIL *follows to above the table.*)

DR. MACPHAIL (*to* MRS. DAVIDSON). Hadn't I better go down to the dock and see what's happening ?

MRS. DAVIDSON. I wish you would.

DR. MACPHAIL. I shall.

(*He exits downstage via the verandah, fanning himself with his hat.*)

(MRS. HORN *enters from the upstage end of the verandah*.)

MRS. HORN (*amiably, coming to* R.C.). Girl kill chicken now—by'n-by you get eating lunch.

MRS. DAVIDSON. Lunch *will* be welcome.

O'HARA (*standing erect*). Here's more company coming, mama !

MRS. HORN (*turning to him*). More company coming ? (*To the upstage end of the verandah step*.) What you say ?

O'HARA. Yeah. More company—I'd say there was.

(PRIVATE GRIGGS *rushes in, from down* R.)

GRIGGS (*on the verandah*). Oh buddy ! You ought to see the dame the *Orduna's* quartermaster's got in tow !—they're both heaving this way—full rigged—all sails set !

(HODGSON *appears and joins* GRIGGS.)

HODGSON. Wait till you see this baby, Tim ! Wait till you see it !

GRIGGS (*whacking* O'HARA *on the back*). Get your prettiest smile on, me hearty—get it on.

O'HARA. Hey, lay off that, or I'll swab the decks with you—what's the matter with you ?

HODGSON (*hugging* O'HARA *and pointing off down* R.). Wait till you see it ! Wait till you see it !

(GRIGGS *and* HODGSON *go into helpless laughter*.)

O'HARA. Stow that, you cubs ! For God's sake act like you had some sense. Are you crazy ?

GRIGGS (*still laughing, and crossing* O'HARA *to above him*). Sure. The heat's gone to our head.

(*Off stage we hear a woman's laughter—shrill, throaty, good-natured, then into the scene comes* MISS SADIE THOMPSON, *hanging on the arm of* QUARTERMASTER BATES *of the S.S. " Orduna."* MISS THOMPSON *is a slim, blondish young woman, very pretty, very cheery, very rakish. She has a tip-tilted nose and merry eyes. She walks easily, without self-consciousness. There is something of the grace of a wild animal in her movements, something primitive perhaps, even as her clothes suggest savage and untutored responses to cut and colour. It is undoubtedly her best hat and frock that she has on. It is the sort of hat and frock a lady of her specie anxious to be taken notice of would wear for appearance at the race tracks in Honolulu or Yokohama or Shanghai. High button shoes,* MISS SADIE THOMPSON *wears, and open-work stockings and she carries a not very new parasol which does not match her dress. When she moves there is a rattling sound, due to the many imitation silver, gold and jade bangles on her wrists. On entering, she pauses and clutches her companion's left arm.* QUARTERMASTER BATES, MISS THOMPSON'S *companion, is a wizened little man with a large moustache. He is several inches shorter than the effulgent* MISS THOMPSON—*but he is blithely unaware of this discrepancy.*

He is highly pleased at the fine figure he believes he cuts, and his whole attitude is that of one who is entirely convinced that he is quite a dashing dog and a devil with the ladies. He twirls his moustache—as MISS THOMPSON *lets go his arm and gestures with her fringy parasol.)*

SADIE (*loudly, as she enters*). So—I'm to be parked here, am I, dearie ? (*She looks about her with bright interest, standing on the verandah step.*)

MRS. DAVIDSON (*in a tense whisper to* MRS. MACPHAIL). That's the girl from the second class he was dancing so outrageously with at the captain's ball last night !

MRS. MACPHAIL. Yes, I thought it rather daring to bring her up to the first cabin, didn't you ?

BATES (*gallantly, to* SADIE, *standing below the verandah step*). Make yourself right at home, Sadie.

SADIE (*clicking her heels together*). I will ! Well, well ! (*She comes in and then turns, pointing with her parasol to the verandah.*) Rail to put one's feet on, 'n everything. (*Seeing the three marines, she does a step of the hornpipe, then waves her parasol at them.*) Ha ! " Join the Navy and see the world." Good boys—that's right—nothing like this where you come from I'll bet.

(*She points to the landscape—the three marines remain speechless—* MRS. HORN *waddles down* R.C.)

BATES (*turning to her*). How de do Mrs. Horn. How's Joe ?

(SADIE *turns to see* MRS. HORN. O'HARA *moves in, to down* R.)

MRS. HORN. Allo Quartermaster ! Joe—he damn fine.
BATES. How's all the kids ? No new ones since my last trip ?

(*He pokes her amiably and winks—at this* MRS. HORN *laughs, highly pleased, and* SADIE *exclaims heartily*)

SADIE (*turning to* BATES). Any of them yours, little honeysuckle ?

(MRS. HORN *and* BATES *find this remark tremendously funny.* MRS. HORN *holds her fat sides with laughter. Between gasps she manages to speak, pointing to* SADIE.)

MRS. HORN. Who is these—mebbe you bring back wife this trip—eh ?
BATES. Get that, Sadie ? She thinks you're my wife—
SADIE (*taking a pace to* MRS. HORN). Say, do I look that weak of intellect, do I look that artless ? Should I marry the little husband of all the world ? No lady, no matter what I am, I'm no pansy stick pin, I broke out of my plush case years ago !

(*At this remark we see the rigid back of* MRS. DAVIDSON *become more rigid.* MRS. MACPHAIL *draws a little closer to* MRS. DAVIDSON. *These two ladies do not speak, but they look volumes.* SADIE *now strolls towards* O'HARA, *who is standing down* R., *apart from his companions. She smiles at him in a friendly way.*)

Hello, Handsome ! When did you leave Kansas ?

(GRIGGS *and* HODGSON, *on the verandah step, howl with laughter.*)

GRIGGS. Ha, ha, the lady's got your number, Tim, it's written all over your map.

HODGSON. Ha, ha ! She got you that time, kid.

SADIE (*turning to* GRIGGS *and* HODGSON, *her hands on her hips*). Say, little high-school boys, cover your books. I was addressing this gentleman. Run back to recess or the girls will get the basketball. (*She turns and observes* O'HARA *shrewdly, offering her hand.*) How are you ?

O'HARA (*shyly, taking her hand*). Fine—very pleased to meet a lady.

(GRIGGS *and* HODGSON *howl.*)

SADIE. What's the matter with these two colts ? (*She regards them severely.*) They act as though they had too much oats. (*She turns to* O'HARA.) I'd ration their feed if I was you—bad thing to jump 'em from milk too fast. Young things like that should be put out to grass first. I'm a farmer's daughter, so I know.

(BATES *howls at this sally, and* GRIGGS *and* HODGSON *look discomfited.* O'HARA *smiles in increasing embarrassment.*)

BATES (*gallantly*). Take a seat, Sadie—make yourself comfortable. Meet these ladies—(*He attempts to lead her over to* MRS. DAVIDSON.)

SADIE (*bringing him up short*). No, little cute one. Now I've got my bearings I think I will go out into the sunshine. Who's coming with me ? (*To* BATES.) You, buttercup ?

BATES. Can't do it, Sadie—I've got to buy some stores for the ship. Why don't one of you boys take Sadie out !

GRIGGS (*on the verandah step*). I am a wonderful little guide.

HODGSON (*on* GRIGGS' R.). Don't believe him, ma'am, I wrote the book he guides by—

SADIE. Yes, I bet you did ! (*Turning to* O'HARA.) I'm taking Handsome—(*crossing and linking her arm in his*). Tag in back if you like but don't get run over. (*To* QUARTERMASTER BATES.) We'll be back for lunch, dearie. Don't forget that swell feed you promised me on shore ? No shark steak or raw eels, please—but all the rest of the atmosphere—and plenty of that cocoanut hooch you mentioned.

BATES. Where are you going, Sadie ?

SADIE. I want to see the cannibals and everything. *A tout a l'heure*, little one—that's French for *au revoir*, if you know the language.

(*She exits with* O'HARA, *down* R., *followed by the marines, waving her parasol as she goes.*)

MRS. HORN (*at* R.C. ; *admiringly to* BATES). Nice, grand lady—who is she ?—Hien ?

BATES (*on her* R., *twirling his moustache*). Friend of mine. Her name is Miss Sadie Thompson.

MRS. HORN. Where she come from ?

BATES. Came aboard at Honolulu—

MRS. HORN. She go Apia ?

BATES. Yeah—got a job down there—cashier in sugar godown—

MRS. HORN. She make change boat here—hien ?

BATES. Yeah, she is waiting for the schooner—you fix us up one tip-top lunch—see ?

MRS. HORN. A'right—I do—(*She starts to exit, nudges him, winks.*) Aw—you davill !

(*She crosses up* L., *and exits into the store.*)

(*During all the above,* MRS. DAVIDSON *and* MRS. MACPHAIL *have been sitting in silence.* MRS. DAVIDSON'S *sharp eyes gleaming behind her pince-nez.* MRS. MACPHAIL *is interested and undecided.* MRS. DAVIDSON'S *long upper lip is tightly pressed against her lower lip, and* MRS. MACPHAIL *from time to time is concerned with the attitude of mind she will be expected to take.* BATES *now approaches them, moving to above the* R. *end of the table.*)

BATES. Well, ladies, I bet you're glad to be on shore again—

MRS. DAVIDSON (*sharply*). We are very well, thank you. Tell me, have you seen Mr. Davidson anywhere ?

BATES. He is aboard the schooner, I think. If I see him, shall I tell him you want him ?

MRS. DAVIDSON. Do not trouble—

BATES. No trouble—I'll be taking Miss Thompson's things over soon.

MRS. DAVIDSON. Miss Thompson ?

BATES. The young lady that was just here.

MRS. DAVIDSON. She was in the second class, wasn't she ?

BATES. Yes—but it'll be all one class to Apia—you'll meet her there—she's full of life.

MRS. DAVIDSON (*dryly*). I believe it !

BATES. If I see Reverend Davidson I shall be glad to—

MRS. DAVIDSON. It will not be necessary—

BATES. Just as you say, ma'am.

MRS. DAVIDSON (*turning her back on* BATES, *and speaking to* MRS. MACPHAIL). I think that we will be more comfortable in those cane chairs . . . (*She rises, followed by* MRS. MACPHAIL, *and sits in the deck-chair.* MRS. MACPHAIL *sits on the chair on her* R.)

(BATES *exits into the store.*)

(*To* MRS. MACPHAIL.) These ship quartermasters are always so dreadfully officious.

(*Note:—During the above conversation it has steadily grown darker.*

A greenish yellow aspect has crept over earth and sky—the clean sunlight of the opening scene has become heavy and turgid. Now the wind begins to moan faintly and a grey pall settles over the scene.)

MRS. MACPHAIL. How dark it's getting—and it is hotter than ever ! *(Fans herself.)*
MRS. DAVIDSON. You must expect it, this time of year.

(Voices are heard off R. *The* REV. DAVIDSON *enters, followed by* DR. MACPHAIL. DAVIDSON *is a man of singular aspect. He is very tall and thin, with long limbs loosely jointed, hollow cheeks and curiously high cheek bones; he has so cadaverous an air that it is a great surprise to note how full and sensual are his lips. He wears his hair very long. His eyes, set deep in thin sockets are large and tragic; his finely shaped hands give him a look of great strength. The most striking thing about him is the feeling he gives of suppressed fire. His is a personality that is impressive and vaguely troubling.* NOTE : *With the entrance of* DAVIDSON *the rain begins to fall, not heavily but lightly, touching the tin roof with a strange sighing refrain. There is a scurry of bare feet on the verandah. The natives appear and start to let down the bamboo rain shutters.)*

MRS. DAVIDSON. What's the matter, Alfred ? Has anything happened ?
REV. DAVIDSON *(clearing his throat)*. Unwelcome news. *(Moving to above and* L. *of the deck-chair.)* We can't start for Apia today.

*(*DR. MACPHAIL *is between the two chairs.)*

MRS. DAVIDSON. Not start today ? *(She rises.)* Why—what—
REV. DAVIDSON *(moving down* L.C., *below the table)*. One of the sailors aboard the schooner has come down with cholera. *(Turning to them.)* We can't sail until it is certain that none of the rest of the crew are affected. It means a delay of several days.
MRS. MACPHAIL *(rising)*. But where can we stay ? Not here, certainly.
REV. DAVIDSON. Here, certainly. There is no other accommodation in Pago Pago. We shall have to be thankful there is a roof over our heads, a bed to sleep on.
MRS. DAVIDSON *(moving to above the* R. *end of the table)*. Can nothing be done ?
REV. DAVIDSON. It is barely possible that I may be able to persuade the Governor to make an exception in our case. *(Crossing to the verandah.)* I am going to see him now.
MRS. DAVIDSON. Take an umbrella, Alfred.
REV. DAVIDSON. No.
(He exits.)
(The others watch him go. MRS. DAVIDSON *sighs deeply.* MRS. MACPHAIL *joins her and looks at her husband weakly.)*

MacPHAIL. I doubt whether he can do much. (*Moving to the table*, L.C.) Peculiar chaps these governors. Their jobs ɔ easy, they have to make them look difficult.

(MRS. MACPHAIL *sits* R. *of the table*.)

MRS. DAVIDSON (*grimly*). Mr. Davidson usually gets what he sets out to get. (*She moves to the verandah and looks out*.)
DR. MACPHAIL (*dryly*). He is luckier than most of us then.

(*Two natives enter from the verandah with boxes of merchandise on their heads. They cross the scene and exit into the trader's store. MRS. DAVIDSON draws back a pace on their appearance*.)

DR. MACPHAIL (*watching them, speaking generally*). A fine race, aren't they ? Make us all look awkward. Notice how their muscles mould into the flesh without one ugly line ?
MRS. DAVIDSON (*moving across to above the table*). I am not an artist, Dr. MacPhail. I am not concerned with their bodies. It is my business to think of their souls. (*Pauses, then says sharply*.) Thank God we have practically eradicated the *lava lava* in our district.
MRS. MACPHAIL. What is that ?
MRS. DAVIDSON. The native costume ! Mr. Davidson thinks that it ought to be prohibited by law. How can you expect a people to be moral when they wear nothing but a strip of cloth around their loins ?
DR. MACPHAIL (*mopping his brow*). Suitable enough for the climate, I should say. (*He turns up, above the chair* L. *of the table*.)

(MRS. MACPHAIL, *troubled, rises and moves slowly down* L., *and turns there as* HORN *enters from the verandah. He is wet, and carries a box of cigars. A native carrying a box of tobacco follows him. The native crosses up* L. *into the store and* HORN *sinks into his rattan deck-chair wearily*.)

HORN. Tough luck for you folks this about the cholera. Looks as though you were in for a stay here. (*He puts the cigars on the stool*.)
DR. MACPHAIL. Any chance of this rain letting up today ?

(MRS. MACPHAIL *moves up and stands by her husband*.)

HORN. Not for long, the rainy season's on, and Pago Pago is about the rainiest place in the Pacific when it rains. Sometimes we don't see the sun for weeks this time of year. You get so used to the infernal downpour you can hear a pin drop.
MRS. DAVIDSON (*breaking in*). We may as well settle about accommodations at once. Have you any rooms that you can let us have ?
HORN. You will want two sleeping rooms, I take it, for your party ?
MRS. DAVIDSON. Yes.

HORN. Best I can do is put you upstairs.

MRS. DAVIDSON. How much will the rooms be ?

HORN. Oh—about four dollars a day, meals included.

MRS. MACPHAIL (*nervously*). Could—could we look at them ?

HORN (*calling, loudly*). Ameena—Ameena !

MRS. HORN (*off* L.). Yes—I come !

MRS. DAVIDSON (*sotto-voce to* DR. *and* MRS. MACPHAIL). Don't expect much, I know what these places are ; we will be lucky if the roof doesn't leak. As for the rest—it is bound to be awful—so don't be disappointed.

(MRS. HORN *enters, from the store, up* L., *and crosses to* R.C.)

HORN. Ah—my spouse. Conduct these ladies upstairs to the— er—royal suite—point out all the comforts and elegances. (*To* MRS. DAVIDSON.) The roof leaks only a little. It is wise of you to resolve not to be disappointed.

MRS. HORN (R. *of the table, addressing* MRS. DAVIDSON *and* MRS. MACPHAIL). All right ladies—I put you in—come 'long— upstairs.

(MRS. HORN *starts upstairs, smiling hospitably.* MRS. DAVIDSON *and* MRS. MACPHAIL *exchange looks and then follow* MRS. HORN. MRS. DAVIDSON *stalks ahead.* MRS. MACPHAIL *draws her skirts carefully about her legs and looks resigned.*)

HORN. Try a cigar. New stock came in today.

DR. MACPHAIL (*moving to* R.C., *above the table*). Thanks—I stick to a pipe. (*He takes out his pipe.*)

HORN (*fumbling under his chair and producing a bottle of square face*). Drink ?

(DR. MACPHAIL *shakes his head.* HORN *pours a drink and smacks his lips.*)

Sightseeing ?

DR. MACPHAIL (*moving down,* R. *of the table*). Not exactly.

HORN (*pausing and regarding* DR. MACPHAIL *with a scrutinizing eye*). You are not a missionary, I can see that.

DR. MACPHAIL (*sitting on the* R. *lower corner of the table*). No, I'm not a missionary—you're right.

HORN. Can't exactly place you, though.

DR. MACPHAIL. I'm a doctor.

HORN. Much better.

DR. MACPHAIL. You sound prejudiced.

HORN. Prejudiced ? Oh no ; damned fine people, missionaries ! Got plenty of good friends among 'em. Some traders are afraid of them, but I've always found 'em all right. My only objection to them is—eh, well they're kind of shy on humour.

DR. MACPHAIL. Is that a necessary qualification for the job ?

HORN. It helps—in any job.

DR. MACPHAIL. Persuading your neighbours to believe what

you believe is a serious business, friend.

HORN (*gulping a drink.*) Gotta have a single track mind for it, anyway.

DR. MACPHAIL. Just so. There's no place for the light touch in reform.

HORN (*spitting a bit of cigar out of his mouth*). That's a word I can't listen to without spitting. It's my belief these reform folk fighting public depravity are only fighting their own hankering for indulgences they suspect others of ! (*He gulps a drink.*)

DR. MACPHAIL (*smiling*). Just so ! They chase you with a hatchet because they'd like a drink too ? Is that it ?

HORN. Shouldn't wonder ! (*Leaning towards* DR. MACPHAIL.) Take these islanders, Doctor ! They're naturally the happiest, most contented people on earth—they asking nothing of life save to be allowed to sing and eat, dance and sleep—thinking gives them a headache—the trees and the sea give 'em all the food they want, so they don't have to fight—they're satisfied with their gods of wind and wave. Then along comes Mr. Missionary in broadcloth and spectacles and tells 'em they're lost souls and have to be saved whether they want to be or not !

DR. MACPHAIL (*reflectively, as he rises and moves down* L.C.). Too bad that man couldn't develop a soul without losing the Garden of Eden . . . (*He turns up* L. *of the table.*)

HORN (*smiling*). You're a real philosopher, Doctor MacPhail.

(SADIE'S *laugh is heard off stage down* R.)

DR. MACPHAIL (*looking across at* HORN). Call me an observer of life, rather !

HORN. Ditto, brother—an observer of life who sees the joke !

(*During the last two speeches we hear, off stage, a succession of staccato squeals and laughing shrill cries. Now* MISS SADIE THOMPSON *comes into view; she rushes across the verandah and into the scene. Close at her elbow is* O'HARA, *and hard at her heels* GRIGGS *and* HODGSON ; *after them hurries* QUARTERMASTER BATES. HORN *turns in his chair to glance at them.* DR. MACPHAIL *watches from above the table.* SADIE *has lifted her skirts above her head to protect her hat from the rain. She stands up* R.C., *laughing and pulling down her dresses. The men, standing on the verandah step, are carrying* SADIE'S *luggage—an oddly assorted multitude of objects hastily thrown together in shawls and large handkerchiefs. There is one very old and battered suitcase.*)

SADIE. Hell ! That was sudden—and me in the only decent togs I've got to my name. (*To her escorts.*) Put that stuff down anywhere, boys.

(*They deposit her luggage at the back of the room and stand wiping the rain from their eyes.*)

Behold—the Wreck of the Hesperus ! (*She crosses down* L., *removing her hat and flicking the ostrich feathers.*) H'm ! That plume has waved its last. Farewell, pretty one—farewell. I guess any idea of me looking neat and chipper when I get to Apia is shot to pieces, eh, what ?

BATES (*crossing to above the* R. *end of the table*). Don't worry, Sadie, you'll dry out.

SADIE (*carelessly*). Shi-cat-a-gani. Shi-cat-a-gani. That's what the Japs in Honolulu say when they mean " I should worry."

BATES (*moving to* HORN). How are you, Joe ?

HORN (*not rising*). Never better, Quartermaster. (*They shake hands.*)

BATES (*to* SADIE, *easing away from the chair*). Shake hands with Joe Horn, Sadie—Miss Sadie Thompson, Joe.

SADIE (*crossing* R., *laughing*). Your climate's bum, Mr. Horn. (*She shakes hands with* HORN, *who rises.*)

HORN. Sorry, it's the best we've got. (*He sits again.*)

SADIE (*between* HORN *and* BATES). Oh, I am not blaming you. What is this about the delay ? How long am I booked for this burg, do you know ?

HORN. Well, I'd compose myself for a two weeks' stay.

SADIE. Two weeks. That being the case, what can't be helped can't be helped, as the canary said when the cat swallowed it.

BATES. Don't fret about that job in Apia, Sadie, they'll keep it for you.

SADIE. I never fret, little one. Make the best of things today— they're bound to be worse tomorrow. (*She turns up* R. *to the marines, in good humour.*) Anyway, I like the boys here.

BATES (*easing towards* HORN). You will find Sadie some place to sleep, won't you, Joe ?

HORN. All the upstairs is let. There's kind of a store-room down here, though. (*Pointing to the door down* L., *covered by bead curtains.*) It is a pretty fair size, and I guess we can rig up a bed.

BATES (*confidentially to* HORN). You know how it is—being short when one is travelling. Sadie left Honolulu kind of sudden—she's a square kid, down on her luck a bit. She can't pay more than a dollar a day. You got to take her for that, Joe.

SADIE (*eagerly*). I was telling the Quartermaster I'll board myself— I got a burner with me. I don't eat so much.

HORN. Oh, that'll be all right. Mrs. Horn will fix you up. Take a look at the room if you like. (*Drinks.*)

SADIE. Much obliged. (*She crosses to the room,* L., *parts the curtains and peeps in.* BATES *crosses to* DR. MACPHAIL, *who has been watching the foregoing scene with quiet amusement.*)

BATES. You and your folks fixed up O.K. ?

DR. MACPHAIL. Yes, we're upstairs. I see the *Orduna's* getting up steam.

BATES. Captain's taking no chance of getting stuck here. We're leaving just as soon as we get our clearance papers.

SADIE (*having peeped into the room, returning*). I'll do fine there. Home with me is where my other pair of shoes is.

BATES (*to* DR. MACPHAIL). You ain't met Miss Sadie Thompson, have you, Doctor.

DR. MACPHAIL. No, I have not had the pleasure.

(SADIE *smiles and bows.*)

BATES. If you get sick, Sadie, yell for Dr. MacPhail.

SADIE (*scornfully*). Get sick ? Never in my life : I'm so healthy that it hurts. Well, now that it's settled where I flop, let's all have a shot of hootch ; I have some rye with me that's not long for this world—it's far too good.

(*Calling to* O'HARA, *who is perched with* GRIGGS *and* HODGSON *on the sofa at the back of the room.*)

Say, Handsome, in that parcel you're resting on you'll find an object tied up in a red handkerchief. Bring it out.

(O'HARA *begins to undo the parcel, which is tied up in a blanket.* DR. MACPHAIL *starts to move to the verandah* ; SADIE *stops him.*)

That includes you, too, Doc. What are you rushing off for ? Seeing we're all stranded here, why not get friendly ?

MACPHAIL (*smiling at her, then moving* R.). Thanks—it is a little early for me. (*To* HORN.) I'll take this umbrella if I may, and meet Davidson.

(*He takes the umbrella in the barrel down* R., *and exits.*)

SADIE (*watching him go*). I'd say that's one wise old bird. (*To* O'HARA.) If the red-eye isn't in that parcel, it's in the brown box.

BATES. You sure are a live wire, Sadie.

SADIE (*moving to above the table*). Oh, I believe in living while one can. We're all going to be a long time dead.

BATES (*to* HORN). Yay Ha ! She sure can stir things up, this kid here, can't she ?

SADIE (*patting* BATES' *shoulder and speaking to* HORN). I suppose I'll find it pretty quiet down in Apia, won't I ?

HORN (*gallantly*). Things ought to brighten up considerable after you get there, anyway !

SADIE (*in a simpery voice*). O-h-h . . . Mis-ter . . . Ho-ho-horn ! (*She winks at him, then turns to* O'HARA.) Say, you are slow ! I'd have thought you'd be thirsty enough to locate by instinct. Here— I'll look. (*She crosses up* R., *and begins to rummage.*)

GRIGGS (*looking over her shoulder as she delves into her belongings*). Twist the devil's tail—if this ain't a gramophone !

SADIE. Yep ! Brought it along for company. Never can tell when one's going to be lonesome.

HODGSON (*delightedly*). Golly. Got any records ?

SADIE. Lots. Wrapped up in my dirty clothes. Hah ! Here's the shy Kentucky refugee. I knew I stowed it safe somewhere. (*She finds the bottle and holds it up.*) Who has a corkscrew ?

(*She returns to the table,* L. *of* BATES. *The marines follow and group above and on her* L.)

BATES (*producing a corkscrew from his pocket*). Now ain't that a purty sight !

SADIE (*handing him the bottle*). Truly very winsome, very winsome, Mr. Bates ! (*To* GRIGGS, *who is taking out the gramophone.*) Look out, Plainfield, that's filled with lingerie.

BATES (*pulling the cork*). Here you are.

(GRIGGS *puts the gramophone on the table and opens it.*)

BATES (*passing the bottle to* SADIE). You first, dearie.

SADIE (*raising the bottle to her lips*). Friend of mine slipped me that before I left Honolulu. " Not that you'll need it, Sadie," said he, " you were born hooched." I sure was ! Why not ? Saves a lot of jack these days.

BATES. No, you sure don't need hootch to pep up.

O'HARA (*at the* L. *end of the table*). I'll find a glass for you, Miss Thompson.

SADIE. Down the hatch ! What for !

(*She takes a swallow, makes a face, coughs, hands bottle to* BATES, *who drinks and hands it to* HORN. GRIGGS *and* HODGSON *are examining the records.*)

GRIGGS (*finding a record*). Holy Willie—" The Wabash Blues ! "

SADIE. Put it on ! Music and a nip of likka—that's what a rainy day is for, says I. (*To* O'HARA.) Can you dance, Handsome ?

(BATES *gets the bottle from* HORN *and passes it to* SADIE, *who passes it to the boys.*)

O'HARA. No, Miss Thompson, I'm a clubfoot ! I never could twist my legs right.

(*The boys take drinks and start the gramophone.*)

SADIE. I'll learn you before I leave—that's a threat. (*Laughs.*) The Quartermaster here is a great stepper. You ought to see him shake a shoulder. For one of his size and years, you'd be surprised. (*To* BATES.) Come on, Ethelbert, and show these island boys how hip meets hip in the gay cafés of Honolulu.

(*The Quartermaster gaily seizes* SADIE *around the waist. He is a little higher than her ears. She puts him in position.*)

BATES. Nothing too fancy now, Sadie.
SADIE. We'll begin trifling and light.

(*They start to dance down* R.C. *and across* L., *below the table, to the huge delight of the marines.* HORN *watches amusedly.*)

GRIGGS. Look—Batesy's one jump ahead of a fit.
HODGSON. One frantic kangaroo !

SADIE (*as they dance at* L.).   Easy there—easy there—whoa.

(MRS. HORN *comes downstairs with a feather duster, watches in amazement, then smiles broadly*.)

Don't bounce—take it easy and smooth—the word to remember is " glide," dearie.   It isn't the dance that counts, it's the rhythm.

(MRS. DAVIDSON *suddenly appears, her eyes dark with disapproval.* MRS. MACPHAIL *follows her.* MRS. DAVIDSON *comes downstage,* R.C. *Then she speaks, doing her best to keep her anger under control*.)

MRS. DAVIDSON.   Young woman . . .

(BATES *hops himself out of step and presently stumbles.* SADIE *pushes him away* L., *ignoring* MRS. DAVIDSON. *The music continues.* HODGSON *throws his hat on the floor and steps forward bravely. He seizes* SADIE *and whirls her about so vehemently that her hair falls down*.)

SADIE (*delightedly, as they dance towards down* C.)   Good news from home !   Batesy, go hide your head.

(*The speed of the dance is accelerated.* MRS. DAVIDSON *now comes determinedly into the scene*.)

MRS. DAVIDSON (*coming toward them*).   Young woman—have you no respect for the Lord's Day ?
SADIE (*without stopping*).   What ?

(*They dance away towards* L.)

MRS. DAVIDSON.   This is Sunday.   Young woman.
SADIE (*slowing up her dance at* L.C. *To* MRS. DAVIDSON).   Were you speaking to me ?
MRS. DAVIDSON.   I am just reminding you that this is the Sabbath.
SADIE (*amiably*).   Let's see, yesterday was Saturday, right you are, sister !   (*She goes on dancing, paying no further attention to* MRS. DAVIDSON.)
MRS. DAVIDSON (*following the dancers*).   I protest !   I protest ! This must stop.   (*They bump into* MRS. DAVIDSON.)
HODGSON.   Are we disturbing you, ma'am ?
MRS. DAVIDSON (*curbing her fury as she fixes on her glasses again*). Whether I have been disturbed or not is of no consequence.   There are six days in the week to dance, if you must dance.   (*Turning to* HORN.)   Is this sort of thing general in your hotel on Sunday, Mr. Horn ?
HORN.   Well, it's a general store, ma'am.
SADIE.   'Nough said—the complaint's registered.   We'll withdraw to my private suite if you've no objection Mr. Horn.
HORN.   No objection—as far as I'm concerned.

SADIE (*to* HORN). Atta nice landlord ! (*To* GRIGGS *and* HODGSON.)
Come on boys, we're moving. (*To* O'HARA.) You take the records,
Handsome. (*To* BATES.) And you, the hooch, little one. (*To* HORN.)
Drop in later, if you feel like it, Mr. Horn—always glad to see you !

(*She crosses to the door, holds back the bead curtain while* O'HARA,
GRIGGS, HODGSON *and* BATES *enter*. MRS. DAVIDSON *stares at*
SADIE *with unwinking expressionless eyes*. SADIE *returns the stare
with saucy amusement, then with a little swagger she exits into
the room, rattling the bead curtains as she goes.* MRS. HORN *exits
up* L., *laughing*. MRS. DAVIDSON *turns sharply on* HORN, *who is
laughing and lounging deep in his chair*.)

MRS. DAVIDSON (R. *of the table, to* HORN). Who is that young
woman ?
HORN (*drinking*). Her name, ma'am, is Thompson, so far as I
know.
MRS. DAVIDSON. I mean—what is she ?
HORN. I didn't enquire. She was on the *Orduna*, wasn't she ?
MRS. DAVIDSON (*biting her lips*). I am aware she was.

(*She turns her back on him and crosses to* MRS. MACPHAIL, *who has
been a meek observer of the scene, standing above the table. From*
SADIE'S *room a ragtime tune now comes bellowing merrily*.)

(*To* MRS. MACPHAIL.) I am afraid that Mr. Davidson will not like
this at all.
MRS. MACPHAIL. I must say that I don't think she is very
suitably dressed.
MRS. DAVIDSON. She is an extremely common woman. I dislike
being under the same roof with her.

(HORN *rises, gives a loud laugh and lounges across* L., *below the
table and off into the store*.)

(MRS. DAVIDSON *watches him go disapprovingly. She turns to*
MRS. MACPHAIL *with set lips. She is very angry*.)

Did you notice—that man was almost insolent ! I tell you on
our island we have the traders trained. A man like this whisky-
bibbing Horn would not be tolerated. Mr. Davidson would drive
him out at once.
MRS. MACPHAIL. How ?
MRS. DAVIDSON (*giving a short laugh and easing away down* R.C.).
You do not know Mr. Davidson. (*Turning*.) There was a man
by the name of Fred Olsen once . . .

(*She stops and smiles.* MRS. MACPHAIL *looks at her inquiringly.*
MRS. DAVIDSON'S *smile increases in grimness*.)

It is a rather long story. I will let Mr. Davidson tell it sometime.

(*The gramophone changes off stage to a wild Spanish Tango.* Mrs.
Davidson *listens with set lips. The record is suddenly removed.*
Mrs. MacPhail *sighs her relief.*)

Mrs. MacPhail.   I'm glad she's stopped that music.
Mrs. Davidson.   She is probably only changing the record.
(*Moving to above the chair* r. *of the table.*)   It didn't take her very
long to get acquainted here, did it ?
Mrs. MacPhail.   Well, you know people of that class aren't
very particular.   I daresay she's harmless enough.

(Mrs. Davidson *gives a short unpleasant laugh.*)

Mrs. Davidson.   I'm not so sure.   I'm not so sure.

(*Off stage are heard the voices of* Rev. Davidson *and* Dr. MacPhail,
who enter. MacPhail *closes the umbrella and puts it in the barrel.*
Davidson *comes toward his wife.*)

Rev. Davidson.   I've argued it out with the Governor but he
says there is nothing to be done.   He is an obstinate man, afraid to
do anything without official sanction.
Mrs. Davidson.   That means ten days here.
Rev. Davidson.   Two weeks probably.
Mrs. Davidson (*sitting above the table*).   Well, I've prepared for
the worst and taken rooms upstairs for us.   Each room is provided
with a chair, a bed and a washstand—we can make out.
Mrs. MacPhail (*sighing*).   But wait until you see the beds,
Robert.   (*She sits at the* l. *end of the table.*)
Mrs. Davidson.   Fortunately there's mosquito netting.   I have
managed to pin together some of the worst rents.   Tomorrow, Mrs.
MacPhail, you and I must sew them.   If we do not, the night will
be unendurable.
Dr. MacPhail (r. *of the deck-chair* r.c.).   Why not today ?
I have no fancy for being eaten up tonight.   (*He sits in the deck-
chair* r.c.)
Mrs. Davidson.   I prefer not to do any sewing on the Sabbath
if I can avoid it.   It would be different if one were indecently exposed
by a tear in one's clothes, for instance, but under the circumstances
it might be a bad example to set before the natives.

(*At this point the gramophone in* Sadie's *room starts again—this
time a very crazy dance record.   There is a sound of laughter and
moving about, not disturbing or loud.* Mr. Davidson *starts,*
Mrs. Davidson *looks apprehensive.   Off stage we hear the siren
of the " Orduna."*)

Rev. Davidson (*putting his finger tips together, moving between
the table and the deck-chair*).   This enforced inactivity is likely to
prove wearisome.   The only thing to do is to portion out the day
to different occupations.

(*The music becomes louder and the noise of voices more penetrating.*
DAVIDSON *checks, listens, then continues.*)

Certain hours each day we had better put aside for study, certain
hours for exercise, rain or shine . . .

(*He pauses; it is evident the music is now irritating him. Again the
" Orduna " siren is heard.*)

Then, too, certain hours must go for recreation.

(*The music crashes. He rises, his lips set, walks to the verandah and
back to the table.*)

DR. MACPHAIL.   Recreation may be hard to find.

(SADIE *laughs loudly in the room* L.)

REV. DAVIDSON.   Someone appears to have found it.

MRS. DAVIDSON (*her eyes on the door* L.).   Yes. That is a person
from the second class—very flashily dressed—exceedingly common.
In fact, she looks rather fast to me. (*Turning to* MR. DAVIDSON.)
Perhaps you noticed her on the boat.

REV. DAVIDSON.   No.

DR. MACPHAIL (*quietly*).   I met her. Rather a good-natured girl,
on her way to a position in Apia.

REV. DAVIDSON.   What kind of a girl ?

DR. MACPHAIL.   Oh, just an ordinary human being—not over
prosperous, I should say.

(*The music becomes a little louder.* DAVIDSON *with an effort controls
a growing irritation.*)

MRS. DAVIDSON (*to* MRS. MACPHAIL).   I must say that I think it
outrageous of her to keep this music up, don't you ? (*She half
rises.*)

REV. DAVIDSON (*quietly, to his wife*), *signing her to sit.* If she
wishes to play her own machine, it is not our right to interfere.

(*Suddenly the music stops.* DAVIDSON *in relief turns to* MACPHAIL.)

By the way, Doctor, I can show you a case of advanced elephantiasis
in the hospital tomorrow, if you're interested.

DR. MACPHAIL.   Um ! A strange disease. Doctors are divided
as to its origin.

(*There is now a sound of singing from* SADIE'S *room.* REV. DAVIDSON
listens. This is followed by laughter and voices. We see that
DAVIDSON *is listening to* DR. MACPHAIL *with only one ear.*)

REV. DAVIDSON (*absently*).   The origin of any disease, doctor, is
overindulgence. (*To his wife.*) There seem to be others in that
room, too !

MRS. DAVIDSON (*indignantly*).   Yes—she has the ship Quartermaster in there, and three or four marines.

(*It is apparent that* DAVIDSON'S *mind is not on what* MACPHAIL *is saying—that he is annoyed and upset by the hub-bub in the next room. There is loud clapping and shuffling.*)

DR. MACPHAIL (*bringing the subject back*). But all nature, Mr. Davidson, is first indulgence, then elimination, is it not ?

REV. DAVIDSON (*above the chair* R. *of the table*). I have no patience with the Darwinian Theory, doctor. In my opinion it should be prohibited by law. (*He stops, and then speaks to his wife.*) This girl, you say, was on the *Orduna* ?

MRS. DAVIDSON (*acidly*). Yes—but Dr. MacPhail has met her— he can tell you more than I can.

DR. MACPHAIL (*impatiently*). She isn't anybody of importance. (*To* DAVIDSON). I am interested, Davidson, in your theory of disease.

REV. DAVIDSON. I believe any disease tendency can be brought under control, just as weakness of the moral structure can. (*Speaking generally.*) Music of this sort is deteriorating, isn't it ?

DR. MACPHAIL. Your theory would be easy, Mr. Davidson, if any of us ever were—ever could be—certain of ourselves.

REV. DAVIDSON (*sharply*). I disagree with you. Why can't we be certain of ourselves ?

DR. MACPHAIL (*coolly*). Because in each and every one of us are hidden blights, erratic formations, undiscovered infirmities. An athlete, seemingly fit as a fiddle, crumples suddenly. Why ? A faulty heart valve gives way ! Not one of us can ever know ourselves until the moment of ultimate pressure—that's the pity of it !

(DR. MACPHAIL'S *speech is cut short by the sharp blast of the " Orduna's " siren.*)

MRS. DAVIDSON. The *Orduna* must be going out before her schedule time.

MRS. MACPHAIL. I sort of hate to have her go. She seems our last link with home somehow !

(*The door of* SADIE'S *room suddenly opens and* BATES *comes unsteadily, adjusting his cap. His step is jaunty, however, and he smiles in vast contentment. From the room beyond comes the sound of laughter and of muffled song.* SADIE *appears at the door.*)

SADIE. Better hurry or you'll get left, little one.

BATES. S-sorry can't wait for l-l-lunch—S-sadie—s-ee you again sometime—you're a good kid.

SADIE. Write me a nice little loving postcard—now don't you forget.

BATES. Sure—nize li'l postcard.

(*He puts his arm around her waist and gives her a resounding kiss.*)

Bye-bye.

SADIE. Toodle-loo.

HORN. Aloha-oa.
SADIE. Sayonara.

(BATES *approaches* MR. *and* MRS. DAVIDSON *and* DR. *and* MRS.
MACPHAIL, *and bows gallantly.* SADIE *stands in the doorway,
watching as he proceeds unsteadily towards* R., *below the table.*)

BATES (*turning at* R.C.). Well, I'm off. Good luck to all you folks.

(*He makes a sweeping gesture with his cap and the " Orduna's "
siren is again heard.*)

REV. DAVIDSON (*decisively*). You had better get aboard,
Quartermaster, as fast as you can.
BATES. Sure, got to be going—must ·get on—gotta hurry—
boat's leaving—bye friends.

(*He moves* R. *jauntily.* SADIE *begins to laugh at his uncertain gait.*
O'HARA *and the other marines appear behind her.*)

SADIE. Look at the list on the little one.
O'HARA (*calling across*). Trim your sails to leeward, old timer,
or you'll founder.
BATES (*turning on the verandah step; singing*).
Way up here in the frozen north,
In the land of the Eski-moo !
I got stranded on the " Sarah Jane "
And I guess I'll never get home again.
The Queen up here is named Gumdrop Sal
And she's mighty fine to me—
The King's in wrong and I'm in right
And the King goes out most every night
And the nights are six months long.

(*During the above, he exits with short, dignified and uncertain steps.*)

(*They wave at him, laughing uproariously.* REV. DAVIDSON *rises and
watches the proceeding with gloomy eyes. Suddenly* SADIE *notices
his eyes are fixed on her. She straightens and a flicker of defiance
crosses her face.* SADIE *and* DAVIDSON *look at one another for
a full, tense moment.* SADIE'S *eyes are the first to drop. She turns
and walks into her room, rattling the curtains as she goes, remarking
in a loud voice:*)

SADIE. A guy out there gave me the dirtiest look !

(*After* SADIE *exits,* REV. DAVIDSON *remains standing, looking at the
door through which she has gone. His eyes are far away, a deep
frown on his forehead. The* MACPHAILS *move restlessly;* MRS.
DAVIDSON *watches her husband anxiously. The rain increases.
On the verandah all the shutters are left down save one, which is
still half-way up. Beyond this we see a gloomy vista of obscured
landscape. There is a moment's silence, broken only by the
monotonous beat of the rain on the tin roof.*)

DR. MACPHAIL. The rain is getting worse. (*Picking up a book from the stool.*)

MRS. MACPHAIL. Yes. Much worse.

REV. DAVIDSON (*moving to the* R. *end of the table, pulling the chair away*). How long has this sort of thing been going on ?

MRS. DAVIDSON. All morning.

REV. DAVIDSON. Where did those sailors come from ?

MRS. DAVIDSON. They just appeared from nowhere, in her wake. If there is to be a fortnight of this, I don't know what we shall all feel like at the end of it.

(REV. DAVIDSON *gives a sudden sharp cry and strikes the table in front of him with his fist.*)

(*Rising.*) Alfred, what's the matter ?

MR. DAVIDSON (*in a dreadful voice*). Of course—it's just occurred to me—the woman's out of Iweili.

MRS. DAVIDSON (*in the same voice*). Iweili—Iweili. (*She turns to* MRS. MACPHAIL *almost triumphantly.*) The thought came to me when I first saw her but I dared not speak of it.

MRS. MACPHAIL. What do you mean by Iweili ?

MRS. DAVIDSON. The plague spot of Honolulu. The Red Light district.

MRS. MACPHAIL (*rising, horrified*). Oh—oh— (*She turns up* L. *of her chair.*)

MRS. DAVIDSON. It is obvious that she has come out here to carry on her trade.

DR. MACPHAIL. I think you're wrong. She had a position waiting for her in Apia.

MR. DAVIDSON. I am not wrong—I know the look of Iweili. One cannot mistake it. I went there once—the faces of its women have haunted me ever since. She is as clearly out of Iweili as though the fact were written in scarlet letters on her brow.

DR. MACPHAIL. Still, one has no right to assume a thing like that unless—

REV. DAVIDSON (*working himself into a state of strange and curious excitement; his lips moving, his fingers twitching*). I tell you that I went there—saw the place—carried away with me the awful memory. Shall I tell you of it ? It lay on the edge of the city. To reach it you went down side streets, near the harbour, in the darkness, across rickety bridges, through deserted roads, then suddenly you came into the light of its shame.

(MRS. MACPHAIL *gives a frightened gasp.*)

DR. MACPHAIL (*quietly*). We can easily imagine the sort of place it was, Davidson.

REV. DAVIDSON. It was the crying scandal of the Pacific, yet it was impossible to avail against it. You know the arguments of the police, that vice is inevitable, consequently the best thing to do is to localise it and control it. The truth is that they were paid—paid !

They were paid by the saloonkeepers, the bullies, paid by the women themselves, but, thank God, at last they were forced by public opinion to do something.

DR. MACPHAIL (*impatiently*). Yes, I read about it in the papers that. came aboard at Honolulu. Politics, wasn't it ?

REV. DAVIDSON. For once a new Mayor dared to live up to his election platform. Iweili with its sin and shame ceased to exist on the day that we arrived in Honolulu. The whole population was brought before the Justice and (*he points to* SADIE'S *door*) this is one who probably managed to escape.

MRS. MACPHAIL (*in a faint voice*). I remember seeing her come aboard just before we sailed. (*She sits again.*) I thought at the time that she had just barely made it—her luggage was tied up in shawls and handkerchiefs.

(MR. DAVIDSON *starts to cross, below the table, towards* SADIE'S *door.*)

MRS. DAVIDSON (*in a low voice ; rising*). Alfred, what are you going to do ?

REV. DAVIDSON (*moving on, to* L.). What do you expect me to do ? (*Turning to them.*) I'm not going to have this house turned into a brothel. I am going to stop her.

DR. MACPHAIL. She has a number of men in there. Isn't it rather rash of you to go in now ?

(DAVIDSON *gives* MACPHAIL *a contemptuous look, but makes no response. He is now at* SADIE'S *door.*)

MRS. DAVIDSON. You know Mr. Davidson very little if you think that fear of physical danger will stop him in the performance of his duties.

(REV. DAVIDSON *opens the door of* SADIE'S *room and stalks in.* MRS. DAVIDSON *gives a little gasp, then clenches her hands tightly. The others sit in tense silence waiting to see what will happen. The singing stops suddenly.*)

SADIE (*off*). I beg your pardon ! What's the idea ?

(*Noise of music screeches and dies away.*)

Hey ! What's going on here ?

(*Noise of gramophone thrown on the floor, and* DAVIDSON'S *voice,* SADIE'S *voice, and those of the marines, viz.,* "Where d'you think you are ? In your own home ? " " Here, quit that ! " *etc., ad lib. Then* DAVIDSON'S *voice louder, and scuffling. A moment later* SADIE'S *door is flung open, and* O'HARA *and* DAVIDSON *appear, struggling.* O'HARA *has* DAVIDSON *by the back of the collar. They lurch on to the stage, and* SADIE'S *angry face appears behind them.*)

SADIE (*shrilly*). Say, the next time you bust into a lady's room maybe you'll get someone to introduce you ! My God ! The nerve of him ! Where does he think he is anyway !

O'HARA.   There—if you know what's good for you, get out and stay out !

(MR. DAVIDSON *falls to the floor, down* L.C.)

(O'HARA *and* SADIE *exit, slamming her door.*)

(*The persons on the stage watch* DAVIDSON *rise. His eyes are terrible. Without a word he turns upstage and starts to mount the stairs very slowly.*)

MRS. DAVIDSON (*calling*).   Alfred—Alfred . . .

(REV. DAVIDSON *makes no answer. He continues upstairs and disappears.*)

MRS. MACPHAIL (*in a scared whisper to* MRS. DAVIDSON).   What will he do ?

MRS. DAVIDSON.   I don't know. All I know is that I would not be in that girl's shoes for anything in the world.

There is a burst of laughter from SADIE'S *room. We again hear voices. The gramophone recommences. We hear the clink of glasses. Someone begins to sing. The three people on the stage sit silent as*

the CURTAIN *falls.*

ACT II

The SCENE *is same as the preceding act. It is late afternoon, two days later.*

It has stopped raining for the time being. On the verandah the rain curtains are drawn half-way up, revealing an angry sullen sky in which a streak of red zig-zags amongst ominous, piled-up clouds. The landscape is indistinct and misty. The gloom of late day is settling over the scene.

As the CURTAIN *rises, we find* HORN, *the trader, asleep in his inevitable cane chair, his face swathed in mosquito netting; by his side is a whisky bottle. From the distance comes the sound of the natives chanting as they drag the fisher nets out of the sea.* HORN's *sleep is restless and uneasy. He squirms and slaps at the mosquitoes which buzz about his head.*

HORN (*muttering*). Pestiferation ! Seize these devils—ur—damnation ! (HORN *strikes out, slaps his ankle, then curses softly and changes his position.*)

(MACPHAIL *enters from the verandah. He comes in to* L. *of the deck-chair and stands looking at* HORN. *He is smoking his usual pipe.* HORN *opens his eyes and wakes slowly, yawning and stretching his arms.*)

Beelzebub and his hosts ! Who—what ! Oh, it's you is it. Hello, Doc !

DR. MACPHAIL. Hello !

HORN (*sleepily*). Been out for a walk ?

DR. MACPHAIL. Only two steps—got as far as the Governor's gate. Like walking through hot pea soup. (*He wipes his moist face with his wide silk handkerchief.*)

HORN (*yawning*). What time of day is it, anyway ?

DR. MACPHAIL (*looking at his watch*). Going on six—whole hour to put in before dinner.

HORN. Been to the hospital today ?

DR. MACPHAIL. No—can't get at my instruments. Nothing left to do, but twiddle my thumbs. (*He sits at the* R. *end of the table.*)

HORN. Why twiddle ? (*He brings the bottle out from under his chair.*)

DR. MACPHAIL. Enforced idleness makes 'em restive !

HORN (*quaffing and smacking his lips*). Native brew—satisfying. What was I saying ?

DR. MACPHAIL. The subject, I believe, was the evil of too much work.

HORN. There's a lot too much misdirected energy in the world, Dr. MacPhail.

B

DR. MACPHAIL (*amused*).   Are you speaking biographically or auto-biographically ?

HORN (*accepting the doctor's joke*).   No, confidentially ! (*He pauses and wags his finger*.) You might as well make up your mind that none of you folks can get away from each other for two weeks— and most of that time it's going to rain like hell ! Don't be too energetic—it starts the throatcutting.

DR. MACPHAIL (*puzzled*).   Throatcutting ?

HORN (*he drinks*).   Just between ourselves, that was a mighty foolish thing the Reverend Davidson did ! That girl Sadie Thompson wasn't doing any harm.

DR. MACPHAIL (*nodding his head*).   Um ! I see what you're getting at.

HORN (*slowly*).   He's been after me for letting her have a room.

DR. MACPHAIL.   It's your own house, isn't it ?

HORN.   Yes. (*Doubtfully*.) But the missionaries are all in with one another. I've never had any trouble with 'em myself, but I know traders that have. If they get down on a trader he may as well shut up shop and quit.

DR. MACPHAIL.   How can that be ?

HORN.   Oh, they have ways.

DR. MACPHAIL.   Surely he isn't asking you to turn this girl out into the rain ?

HORN.   No—not exactly. He knows there'd be no place for her to go except a native hut. Not but what I think she'd do better to go into one than stay here, now that he is on to her.

DR. MACPHAIL.   Just what *does* he want you to do ?

HORN.   He said he wanted to be fair to her and to me, but he wouldn't stand for any " doings."

DR. MACPHAIL.   Er—what do you think, Horn—is she—er—out of Iweili, that Honolulu red light district ?

HORN (*complacently*).   I don't know. And I don't care. (*He looks up at* MACPHAIL.) What if she is ? We've all crossed thresholds we don't brag about.

(MACPHAIL *gives a slight cough as the truth of this statement reaches him and somewhat embarrasses him. He starts to cross back to his seat by the table, then pauses in his walk and listens intently as* HORN *continues*.)

Just because she has a few gaudy rags and a bum gramophone, what right has he to conclude that she's out of Iweili ? You know, Dr. MacPhail, the whole trick in thinking is, what vision have you. (*Pauses*.) If you have a low horizon, God pity you ! Davidson has that ! (*He waves his hand in a deprecatory manner*.) This girl hasn't any—that's why I like her. Poor thing ! Davidson's sort of got her wondering.

DR. MACPHAIL.   How so ?

HORN.   She's wondering what he's up to ! You noticed when

the boys came around last night to see her, she got them out on
the porch pretty quick and talked to them there ?
DR. MACPHAIL (*dryly*). Yes—I noticed ! It wasn't the most
cheerful of evenings either ! (*Rising and moving up* R., *looking off.*)
What with the rain and everything, we'd all been happier, I think,
if Miss Thompson had been in her room with her friends.
HORN. She felt it too, I guess. (*Examining the contents of his
cigar box.*) I hear she went to a half-caste family this morning and
tried to get 'em to take her in, but they wouldn't.
DR. MACPHAIL. Why not ? (*He comes down,* L. *of* HORN'S *chair.*)
HORN (*succinctly, taking a cigar and closing the box*). Afraid to !
Must have heard somewhere that the missionaries had got their
knives in her. (*He pauses; then continues in confidence.*) Maybe
you don't know, but he's been at the Governor to have her sent
back to the States. (*He lights his cigar.*)
DR. MACPHAIL (*removing his pipe*). I thought he was up to
something like that.
HORN. Yeah, he's got his mind made up to get her out of these
islands, no matter what ! And she's got wind of it somehow, too !
DR. MACPHAIL (*slowly; moving to* L.C., *above the table*). You
know I felt rather sorry for her last night. After her sailor friends
left she went into her room without looking at any of us. Just
as we were ready for bed she put on her gramophone. Somehow it
sounded dismal—like a cry for help.

(*At this moment from* MISS THOMPSON'S *room comes the sound of
the gramophone—shrill, discordant, as though put on as a final
resort.* HORN *and* MACPHAIL *listen.* HORN *points to* MISS
THOMPSON'S *room, puts his finger to his lips and shrugs his shoulders.*
MACPHAIL *changes his position slightly. They both listen. There
is a moment's silence. Suddenly the record is snatched off and
another is substituted.*)

HORN. There it goes again !
DR. MACPHAIL (*moving down* L. *of the table, to below it, and
sitting*). Hard business, trying to cheat one's loneliness.
HORN. Take it from me, she's scared as well as lonely ! Not
that she'd show it—she's got nerve ! But she don't know what
Davidson's doing and it makes her anxious. Where is he now,
anyway ?
DR. MACPHAIL. He's been coming and going from the Governor's
all afternoon—whatever that may mean. (*He knocks the ashes
from his pipe suddenly as the rain begins to patter lightly on the iron
roof.*)
HORN. You're jumpy.
DR. MACPHAIL. Maybe. This rain—it's starting up again.
HORN. Yes, it goes on pretty steady in the rainy season. We
have three hundred inches in the year—it's the shape of the bay.
DR. MACPHAIL. Damn the shape of the bay ! (*He rises and*

stalks to the verandah and back to up R.C., *then back to the verandah again*.)

HORN (*regarding him in amusement*). It's getting you !—all this lush, dripping world—outside, everything growing with a sort of savage violence ! Tomorrow you will see strange flowers where yesterday there were only roots. For myself I like it. This rain you hate—it wipes out, it kills—and it begins . . .

(*During the above speech the gramophone stops.* MACPHAIL *move down* R. *The bead curtains outside* SADIE'S *room part and she enters, in a sudden nervous way. She wears a not very new dress of limp red gingham. There is considerable cotton lace about the dress, which is the sort of garment one might see in a third-rate department store window devoted to summer styles. Around her neck she wears a string of cheap beads. She affects a brave assumption of cheer and good fellowship*.)

SADIE. Evening, everybody ! My, the merry water sprites sure do carry on, don't they ?

(MACPHAIL *nods a little embarrassedly.* HORN *salutes with gallantry.* SADIE *smiles at both in a friendly manner. She comes forward, fanning herself.*)

Don't let's mention the heat. Let's talk of Greenland's icy mountains !

(*Neither* MACPHAIL *nor* HORN *speaks and* SADIE *continues, trying hard to keep up her good cheer, moving below the table to* R. *of it.*)

You don't mind, do you, seeing we're here by ourselves, if I sit down with you boys and have a smoke ? (*She takes out a cigarette and lights it.*)

HORN. Sure. Sit down, light up.

SADIE (*seating herself in the chair* R. *of the table*). You haven't seen that Marine Sergeant I call Handsome 'round anywhere today, have you.

HORN. No—he hasn't been around today.

SADIE. It don't matter. I just wanted to ask him something. If you do see him, tell him to drop around this evening.

HORN. I—er—er—you know what I said to you last night ?

(SADIE *nods.*)

As friend to friend, get me ? I'd go slow on company for a day or two.

SADIE. I see. Until Reverend Davidson gets over his terrible experience, eh ? (*She gives a short laugh.*) You'd think I'd been to blame for what happened.

HORN. I'm not blaming anyone.

SADIE. What else could he expect, that Reverend Davidson, pushing himself in on us in that way. It's a wonder one of the boys didn't show him what a real crack is ! As it was they only handed him a love tap and hustled him out. He's a great missionary, I'll announce, if he's trying to take it out on us just because he got what was coming to him. (*She continues working herself up to a sense of lively indignation.*) What harm were we doing ? Just talking and singing'—everything happy and pleasant, then bang went the door and in came Reverend Davidson, and began to bawl us all out. The boys thought he'd just naturally gone crazy, so they put the skids under him.

(HORN (*soothingly*). I know . . . Anyway, I wouldn't attract his attention any more than I had to, just now.

(MACPHAIL *eases quietly upstage by the verandah steps, to watch.*)

SADIE (*indignantly*). Attract his attention ! Well, if it comes to that, he'd better not attract mine ! I've never known anyone like him and I don't want to ! (*She pauses, then asks confidentially.*) Say, what kind of an egg is the Governor of this place ?

HORN. The Governor ? Let's see. Pretty good sort, I'd say. Why ?

SADIE. I just wanted to know, that's all. The nerve of that Reverend Davidson going to see him about me ! Did you ever hear the like of it ?

HORN. How do you know Davidson went to see the Governor about you ?

SADIE. O'Hara told me. He's reported O'Hara to his officer for drinking. I don't want that boy to get into trouble through me.

HORN. Oh, I guess O'Hara can take care of himself.

SADIE (*rising*). Well, so can I, if it comes to that ! (*Moving towards* HORN; *angrily.*) If that Davidson gets gay with me again, I'll tell him who his mother was. Possibly he don't know ! (*She gives a loud, derisive laugh.*)

HORN. Miss Thompson—I'd be careful . . .

SADIE. Of what ?

HORN. I'd be careful for my own good. One can't tell what . . .

SADIE (*impatiently, moving away to* C.). God give me strength ! (*Turning to* HORN.) How many times have I got to tell you that old sin buster doesn't mean a thing to me. If he minds his own business, I'll mind mine, and if he's looking for trouble, I'll see he gets it ! That's all ! (*She stops suddenly and cups her hand over her ear.*) Methinks I hear the winds of religion whistling down the chimney !

(*Voices are heard off stage;* SADIE *moves away* L. *with mock trepidation.*)

Whereat the low hussy frolics off to buy her dinner ! (*Turning at* L., *to* HORN.) Where do you keep your tomales, old partner ?

HORN. If there's any left, they're on the shelf by the door.

(SADIE *crosses up to the door of the store with an attempt at rakishness, then pauses and looks back at* HORN *and* MACPHAIL *a little doubtfully.*)

SADIE.   Anyway, there's no ill feeling between any of us, is there ?
(*To* MACPHAIL.) The doctor hasn't been saying much. (*She shrugs
her shoulders, then laughs nervously.*) Life just teems with quiet fun,
don't it ?

(*She exits into the store.*)

(MACPHAIL *moves towards the* R. *end of thé table.*)

HORN (*to* MACPHAIL).   There—what did I tell you ?   She's
frightened.

(MACPHAIL *sighs and does not respond.*   HORN *rises and moves
slowly* L., *below the table.*)

(*There is an increased patter of rain on the roof, and the scene darkens.
Two natives appear on the verandah and begin to draw the shutters.
There is a moment's silence during which we hear only the rain and
the slip-slop of native feet and the low murmur of their voices.
Then* MRS. DAVIDSON *enters from outside, followed by* MRS.
MACPHAIL.*)

MRS. DAVIDSON (*to* HORN).   Has Mr. Davidson arrived ?

HORN (*turning up* L.).   No, ma'am.

(*He exits into the store.*)

DR. MACPHAIL (*moving down* L., *below the table*).   How far did
you ladies go ?

MRS. MACPHAIL (*crossing to* C., *above the table*).   Only as far as
the wharf. We watched the clouds pile up. Such curious black
shapes as they were taking. I got a little afraid. So Mrs. Davidson
thought we'd better get back. (*She sits, above the table.*)

DR. MACPHAIL (*to* MRS. DAVIDSON.) How's the headache ? Any
better ?

MRS. DAVIDSON.   Very little. (*She sits,* R. *of the table.*)   Mr.
Davidson has had no sleep for two nights. When he doesn't sleep,
I cannot sleep. At four this morning he got up and got dressed
and went out. He came back wet through, but he wouldn't change.
(*She sighs.*) It's that thing that happened the other day ! It's
preying on his mind.

DR. MACPHAIL (*sitting* L. *of the table*).   She—that girl—Miss
Thompson was in here just before you came. I think—I have an
idea she is sorry for what happened. I am sure she could be easily
persuaded to apologize.

MRS. DAVIDSON.   There is no question of apology. I do not
know what will happen. I know only this. He will conquer this
girl, perhaps quickly, perhaps slowly—but in the end completely.

(SADIE *enters from the trader's store, talking to* HORN, *who enters
with her. She is carrying a can of tomales and a pitcher.* HORN
follows her. MRS. DAVIDSON *gives* SADIE *a swift look, then speaks
to* MRS. MACPHAIL.*)

Do not look around ! Here she comes now !

SADIE (*moving down* L., *flushing with anger*). Yes, here I come now !
Why shouldn't I come now ? See here, let's settle this. I'm paying
for my own room with the privilege of getting my own meals. Is
that so, Mr. Horn ?

HORN (*down* L., R. *of* SADIE, *anxious to escape the scene*). That's
so, Miss Thompson.

SADIE. Then will you kindly tell these ladies I have as good
a right here as they have ?

HORN. Now, Miss Thompson, there isn't anyone saying you
haven't.

(*He pats her soothingly and exits into the store.*)

MRS. DAVIDSON (*to* MRS. MACPHAIL). Don't look at her—don't
speak to her.

SADIE. No—I wouldn't if I were you. But seeing you started
the conversation by talking at me, I may as well be polite. How's
your husband today ? If I may say so, he wasn't looking any too
well when I saw him gumshoeing down the road this morning.

DR. MACPHAIL. Miss Thompson, please . . .

SADIE (*viciously*). What your husband needs, I think, is a good
dose of salts ! (*She turns down to her door.*)

MRS. DAVIDSON (*in a voice choking with fury*). Don't you dare
speak to us again, you dreadful woman ! If you insult me I shall
have you turned out of here . . .

SADIE (*turning at her door*). Say ! Did I ask Mr. Davidson to
make my acquaintance in the first place ? Did I ?

MRS. MACPHAIL. Don't answer her !

SADIE. I assure you the overtures to know *me* have been entirely
on your side of the fence !

(*She exits, closing her door with a bang.*)

MRS. DAVIDSON. She's brazen—outrageous ! (*She puts her
hands to her head as though about to choke.*)

MRS. MACPHAIL (*rising and going to her*). Don't. You'll only
harm yourself—ånd all for that creature. (*Turning towards*
MACPHAIL.) Robert—

MRS. DAVIDSON (*feebly*). It's foolish, I know, but this is the first
time I have ever had words with a woman of that sort. Well, there's
one comfort, we shan't have to suffer this sort of thing much longer !
(*She smiles in rather a grim and terrible manner.*) No ! Mr.
Davidson is attending to that !

MRS. MACPHAIL (*curiously*). What do you suppose he is doing ?

MRS. DAVIDSON. When Mr. Davidson is on the Lord's work
I do not question him.

(MRS. DAVIDSON *clenches and unclenches her hands.* MRS. HORN
*enters from the store with a lamp which she takes to the table
upstage by the sofa, and lights it.*)

MRS. HORN. Dinner soon now—mebbe one hour—one hour half. (*She crosses back to the door up* L.)

MRS. DAVIDSON (*sighing*). I only hope I can persuade Mr. Davidson to eat something tonight.

(MRS. HORN *exits*.)

MRS. MACPHAIL. He doesn't think of himself at all, does he ?

MRS. DAVIDSON (*slowly, tensely*). Never ! He is so without thought or fear for himself that often he is like a man possessed.

(MACPHAIL *has been sitting quietly during the above conversation— a somewhat quizzical expression on his face. Now he jerks himself forward in his chair suddenly and strikes at his ankle*.)

DR. MACPHAIL. Damn those mosquitoes !

MRS. MACPHAIL (*reprovingly*). Robert ! (*She moves to* L. *of the chair above the table*.)

DR. MACPHAIL. Sorry ! I've always been touchy about the ankles ! They seem to know it !

(*He looks off and sees* DAVIDSON *approaching*.)

Hello, Davidson.

(DAVIDSON *enters, coming into the room from the porch. He shakes the rain from his hat and removes an oilskin cape*.)

MRS. DAVIDSON (*rising and going to him at* R.). Alfred, please change your wet clothes !

REV. DAVIDSON (*crossing her, to up* R.C.). No—I shall be going out again probably.

MRS. DAVIDSON. Again ! Oh you must try to get a little rest. Alfred—you must ! (*She sits in the deck-chair*.)

REV. DAVIDSON (*almost tenderly, turning to her*). My wife, like Martha, " thou hast troubled thyself about many things "—and mostly about me ! (*He smiles but his eyes are far away; then he turns, speaking to* MACPHAIL.) I do not know what I could ever have done without my dear wife. In the early days of our island ministry when my heart sank and I was near despair it was she who gave me strength and courage to go on. It was she who put her work aside and read to me from the Bible until peace came and settled upon me like sleep upon the eyelids of a child—and when at last she closed the book, she would say, " we will save them in spite of themselves ! " Then I would feel strong again and answer, " Yes, with God's help I will save them. I must save them ! "

(*During the above*, MRS. DAVIDSON *is deeply affected, too. She takes off her glasses and wipes them, she holds back her tears with a great effort*.)

DR. MACPHAIL (*dryly*). Save who ?

MRS. MACPHAIL (*quickly*). The islanders, Robert ! (*She moves to* R. *of the table and sits*.)

(*From* SADIE THOMPSON'S *room comes the sound of the gramophone—harsh, wheezy.* DAVIDSON *listens.* MRS. MACPHAIL *looks nervous.* MRS. DAVIDSON *bites her lips.* DR. MACPHAIL *puffs his pipe.*)

MRS. DAVIDSON (*To* DAVIDSON). Alfred, just before you got back that girl was in here ; she jeered and screamed at us. What are you going to do about her ?

REV. DAVIDSON (*putting his hand to his temple*). I must give her every chance first—every chance—before I act.

(MRS HORN *enters with a tray of dinner dishes, which she places on the table, after first laying down the slovenly cloth.*)

DR. MACPHAIL. Hamburg steak tonight again, Mrs. Horn ?

MRS. HORN (*clattering the dishes*). Hamburg steak, I give you —bananas fried—mebbe.

DR. MACPHAIL (*gloomily*). Strange how one's thoughts run to food when there is nothing else to think of.

REV. DAVIDSON. As it happens, there is a great deal to think of. (*To* MRS. DAVIDSON.) You say this Thompson woman spoke to you ?

MRS. DAVIDSON. She thrust herself in upon us with low insults.

REV. DAVIDSON. H'm ! The Governor tells me the affair is no concern of his, but if I find her incorrigible I shall see to it he *acts.* I am afraid he has no backbone.

DR. MACPHAIL (*attempting facetiousness*). I suppose that means he won't do exactly as you want—whatever it is you want him to do ?

REV. DAVIDSON. I only want him to do what is right !

DR. MACPHAIL (*laconically*). There may be differences of opinion about what is right.

REV. DAVIDSON. If a man had a gangrenous foot, would you have patience with anyone who hesitated to cut it off ?

DR. MACPHAIL. But gangrene is a matter of fact . . .

REV. DAVIDSON. And is not evil ?

DR. MACPHAIL (*quietly*). To me it has always seemed a matter of opinion. Anyway the poor thing will only be here until the boat for Apia goes.

REV. DAVIDSON. And after she gets to Apia ?

DR. MACPHAIL. I can't see how that concerns us.

REV. DAVIDSON (*moving to above the chair* R. *of the table*). That's where you and I differ. (*He stops, looks hard at* MACPHAIL *and continues.*) You don't mind my turning you out of here for a little while, do you ? I want to speak to this woman alone. (*To* MRS. DAVIDSON.) I think it would be best if you went too.

(DR. *and* MRS. MACPHAIL *rise silently, cross* R., *and disappear along the verandah, upstage.*)

MRS. DAVIDSON. Alfred, why do you see her ?

REV. DAVIDSON. I cannot act until I've given her every chance.

MRS. DAVIDSON. She'll insult you.

REV. DAVIDSON. Let her insult me. Let her spit on me. She has an immortal soul and I must do all that is in my power to save it.

(*During the above scene* MRS. HORN *has been busy at the table.*
DAVIDSON *now turns to her and speaks.*)

Ask Miss Thompson if she will step out of her room for a moment.
    MRS. HORN (*coming forward*).   You want spik with Miss
Thompson ? (*She points to* SADIE'S *room.*)
    REV. DAVIDSON.   Yes.   Ask her to kindly come out for a
minute.
    MRS. DAVIDSON.   I tell you, Alfred, she has gone too far.
    REV. DAVIDSON.   Too far for the mercy of the Lord ? (*His
eyes light up and his voice grows mellow and soft.*) Never ! The sinner
may be deeper in sin than the depth of hell itself, but the love of
the Lord Jesus can reach him still.

(MRS. DAVIDSON *turns and goes out upstairs.*)
(MRS. HORN *knocks on* SADIE'S *door.* SADIE *answers,* " Come."
    The music stops and after a moment enters.)

    SADIE (*moving down* L., *munching a banana*).   What is it ? (*She
looks enquiringly at* MRS. HORN, *who points with her thumb to where*
DAVIDSON *stands.*)
    MRS. HORN.   He wan make talk wit you.

(MRS. HORN *exits into the store.*)

SADIE *half hesitates* (*on seeing* DAVIDSON, *then squares her shoulders
    and stands against the doorway, her eyes fixed on him.*)

    SADIE (*to* DAVIDSON).   You want to see me ?
    REV. DAVIDSON.   Yes, I want to talk to you, Miss Thompson.
    SADIE.   I'm eating my supper. (*He mouth is full of banana.*)
    REV. DAVIDSON.   I'll wait until you're through.
    SADIE.   Oh, the supper can stand by if it's important.
    REV. DAVIDSON.   It is important—very important.

(SADIE *comes forward, her eyes on* DAVIDSON. *He motions her to
    a seat. She sits nervously,* L. *of the table. He stands looking at
    her strangely.*)

Sadie Thompson, I have brought you out here to make you a gift—
the most precious gift life can offer you.
    SADIE (*uncertainly*).   You want to give me something ?
    REV. DAVIDSON.   The gift I offer is free.
    SADIE (*with a nervous titter*).   I'm glad of that. I'm pretty short
on cash. (*She throws the banana skin on the table.*)
    REV. DAVIDSON (*moving to below the chair* R. *of the table*).   The
gift I'm offering you is the infinite mercy of our Lord Jesus Christ.
    SADIE (*suspiciously*).   Just what is the idea, Reverend Davidson—
making me these presents ?
    REV. DAVIDSON.   The time has come, Sadie Thompson, for you
to make your choice. The broad bosom of our Lord, His tender
arms, His all consoling whisper in your ear, His healing fingers on
your weary eyes—all these are yours for the asking.

SADIE (*with dignity*).   I don't know why I get all this attention from you, Reverend Davidson.   I guess you mean well, but I think I can worry along just as I've been worrying along these several years without your help.   I go my own way and don't ask any favours.

REV. DAVIDSON (*pleasantly*).   Those who have the key of salvation offered them, and fail to open that door, must be destroyed.

SADIE (*cheerfully*).   I see what you mean !   But I won't get destroyed.   I always make out one way or another !   (*She rises.*) If that's all, Reverend Davidson, I guess I'll go back and eat— I'm hungry.   (*She moves away* L.)

REV. DAVIDSON.   You are hungry for the bread of the Spirit. You are thirsty for the waters of eternal life.

SADIE (*turning*).   You mean right by me, Reverend Davidson— and I sure am grateful, especially after what happened the other day.   (*She comes towards him in a half shy, half confidential manner.*) You know, just between ourselves, I had sort of a feeling you were laying to get me for that little trouble we had—you know !   When you busted the gramophone and the boys bawled you out.   I felt awful bad about it   I've been wanting to apologize.

REV. DAVIDSON (*patiently*).   You are mistaking me—but I do not think wilfully.

SADIE (*below the chair* L. *of the table*).   They all told me you were sore, but I just couldn't think a man as big as you would hold a grudge over a little misunderstanding.

REV. DAVIDSON.   All this is beside the point, Miss Thompson. The only thing that concerns me now is that you must be given your chance before I act.

SADIE.   My chance for what ?

REV. DAVIDSON.   Your chance to be saved.

SADIE (*carelessly, sitting against the lower edge of the table*). Oh, I'm all right—don't you bother about me a bit !   You see (*she smiles in a frank, friendly manner*) I'm a happy-go-lucky kind of a fellow !   I'll be all right as soon as I get to Apia.   I've got friends there.

REV. DAVIDSON (*slowly*).   You have friends in Apia ?   What sort of friends ?

SADIE.   Oh, just friends !   A girl I used to work with is there. She wrote me I could have a job as cashier.   I'm pretty quick at figures.

REV. DAVIDSON.   For some time past you have lived in Honolulu, haven't you ?   What did you do there ?

SADIE (*evasively*).   Well, part of the time I had sort of a singing job.   (*She smiles.*)   My voice isn't so awful if you don't listen too hard.

REV. DAVIDSON.   Before you went to Honolulu, where were you ?

SADIE.   Where do I come from, do you mean ?

(*Their eyes meet.   He regards her gloomily.   She forces herself to*

*return his stare. Her nervousness reveals itself in the tensity of
her fingers as they twist the dress she wears.*)

I was born in Keneshaw, Kansas—if that means anything—but pa
and ma got the California fever, so they sold the farm and bought
a little ranch outside Los Angeles. I was about fifteen then I guess.
Then ma died and pa and I didn't get along so well, so I went up
to San Francisco. I was working there up to the time I went to
Honolulu . . .

REV. DAVIDSON. What made you go away to Honolulu ?

SADIE (*nervously*).   I—I don't know.   I wanted a change I
suppose . . .

REV. DAVIDSON. Ah ! You wanted a change. Well, Sadie
Thompson . . . (*There is a long pause in which* DAVIDSON'S *gloomy
eyes seem to chisel into* SADIE'S *soul.*) This gift I offer you—what
are you going to do about it ?

SADIE. Do about it ? I don't know. I don't know what you're
talking about ! I can take care of myself. Up or down—in jack or
broke ! What's the odds ? Wherever night overtakes me, that's
my resting place—that's my way. (*She rises and eases* L., *then turns
to him.*) Thank you for your interest, though—it's kind of you
after what happened. I'm mighty glad you aren't sore at me. I like
to keep friends with everybody.

REV. DAVIDSON (*firmly*). Sit down, Miss Thompson, I see I must
be very patient.

(SADIE *sits,* L. *of the table.*)

I see I must make you understand. My poor lost child, what
happened the other day is of no importance. Do you imagine what
you or those sailors said to me made any difference ?

SADIE (*greatly relieved*). You certainly are all to the good, Mr.
Davidson, and I want to say this. Don't be afraid but that I'll
keep to myself. I know oil and water don't mix. The ladies in your
party won't even know I'm under the same roof with them. I'll
be as quiet as a mouse ! (*She rises and moves down* L.)

REV. DAVIDSON (*firmly, moving to below the table*). Don't go,
Miss Thompson. You must listen to me.

SADIE (*wearily, moving past him to down* R.C.). Reverend Davidson
—*why* do you worry about me.

REV. DAVIDSON (*moving up, by the chair* R. *of the table*). You've
had your own soul in trust and you failed. It is now my business to
show you the way to redeem it.

SADIE (*turning at* R.C.). And haven't I anything to say about
myself then ?

REV. DAVIDSON. Yes—you can choose one of two paths.

SADIE (*with a flash of " pep "*). What's second choice ?

REV. DAVIDSON (*in a final voice.*) Destruction !

SADIE. And who's going to destruct me ?

REV. DAVIDSON. The forces which find no place for evil.

SADIE (*in a half whisper*). And you—what are you going to do ?
REV. DAVIDSON. Only my duty.
SADIE. What might that be ?
REV. DAVIDSON. Infectious diseases must be quarantined. Sin must be segregated until it can be stamped out.

(*A long look passes between them; an expression of terror comes into* SADIE'S *eyes. She backs down against the deck-chair like an animal at bay.*)

SADIE (*shrilly*). I know ; you went to see the Governor about me, didn't you ? Oh, don't say you didn't. I got it straight. Some of the boys told me. They didn't know what you said, but they told me to look out for you ! Now I understand what they meant.
REV. DAVIDSON. You are right. I have been to the Governor. (*Rushing along.*) I shall not let you go to Apia, Sadie Thompson. You are an evil woman, you have lived an evil life. You have come here only to carry your infamy to other places. You are a harlot out of Iweili !
SADIE. You're a liar !
REV. DAVIDSON (*moving down nearly level with* SADIE, *on her* L.). Look at me.
SADIE. Who the hell do you think you are—standing there, calling names !
REV. DAVIDSON. Look at me. Do you deny that you escaped from Iweili ?
SADIE (*hysterically*). I've listened all I'm going to listen to you. Now you listen to me. You just told me to be careful. Be careful yourself ! Lay off me or I'll show you what it means when I start to get mad. It'll be the worse for you, if you don't.
REV. DAVIDSON. The devil in you is strong, poor Sadie Thompson. Evil has claimed you as its own.
SADIE. You take care of your own evil, and I'll take care of mine. (*With a horrid laugh.*) I know what you want ! You want another scalp to hand to the Lord. Well, you don't get mine, old tit-bit !
REV. DAVIDSON (*passionately breaking in*). Lord !—Hear Thou my prayer for this lost sister. Close Thy ears to her wild and heedless words. (*He puts his hand on her arm. She draws it away.*)
SADIE. You Bible backs don't fool me. I've met you before ! Make me go over your way, would you ? Just try it !

(DAVIDSON *grasps her arm and tries to force her to kneel.*)

REV. DAVIDSON. Kneel, Sadie Thompson, God is waiting. He is waiting.
SADIE (*pulling away*). You let go of me !
REV. DAVIDSON (*reaching for her*). This is your last chance, Sadie Thompson. Kneel with me and pray.

(He grabs her wrist. She allows him to hold it for a second. She looks right into his eyes. Then she gives a peal of sudden laughter and tosses his hold away from her wrist.)

SADIE *(crossing him quickly to* C.*)*. Oh-h ! You make me laugh !
REV. DAVIDSON *(in an awful voice)*. Sadie Thompson, you're doomed !

*(*SADIE *turns to him. For a moment they face each other. Again* SADIE *laughs; then suddenly she spits full in* DAVIDSON'S *face, turns, rushes into her room and slams the door, leaving* DAVIDSON *alone.* DAVIDSON'S *eyes are dark and fearful and his hands work convulsively. He breathes heavily.* MRS. DAVIDSON *comes hastily down the stairs.)*

MRS. DAVIDSON *(moving down to above the* R. *end of the table)*. Alfred ! What happened ?

*(*DAVIDSON *slowly turns up toward his wife.)*

REV. DAVIDSON *(in an awesome voice)*. I have given her every chance. I have exhorted her to repent. Now, I shall take the whips with which the Lord Jesus drove the usurers and the money changers out of the temple of the Most High.

(He paces R. *and back in wild exaltation. His wife watches him in fear.)*

Even if she fled to the uttermost parts of the earth, I should pursue her !

(He picks up his hat and goes R. *The gramophone in* SADIE'S *room breaks into the " Dance of the Marionettes.")*

MRS. DAVIDSON *(taking a step after him)*. Alfred !

*(*DAVIDSON *does not heed her. He stalks out* R.*)*

(She makes a futile gesture, then, ignored and hurt, she stands irresolute.)
Alfred !

(As she says this, she sinks into a chair, her hands clasped uselessly in her lap. O'HARA *enters through the verandah. Having just collided with the unseeing* DAVIDSON, *he rubs his shoulder and smiles.)*

O'HARA *(moving to* R.C.*)*. There was *some* big breeze ! *(On seeing* MRS. DAVIDSON, *he stops and mumbles.)* Evening !

*(*MRS. DAVIDSON *turns on hearing* O'HARA. *She rises and faces him. Once more she is the missionary. This is her chance to do something. She is alert and brisk.)*

MRS. DAVIDSON. Young man, I should not come here if I were you.

O'Hara. Why ?

Mrs. Davidson. You are likely to get into more trouble than you're in already !

O'Hara. This isn't my first year away from home ma'am— and I haven't got run over yet !

Mrs. Davidson. Do you know what kind of a girl this Sadie Thompson is ?

O'Hara. I don't ask anything of anybody except to be square.

(Sadie's *door opens and* Sadie *comes out. She stops, standing in her doorway.*)

Mrs. Davidson. My advice to you is, keep away from bad company !

Sadie (*breaking in on* Mrs. Davidson). Bad company ! (*She salutes and clicks her heels.*) Present !

(Mrs. Davidson *gives* Sadie *a look of withering disgust. Then she turns and without a word marches upstairs.*)

(Sadie *and* O'Hara *watch her until she is out of sight. Then* Sadie *turns to* O'Hara *and snaps her fingers with a weary gesture.*)

Such is joy ! (*Her expression changes as she sinks into the chair* R. *of the table with a bitter sigh.*)

O'Hara (*to* Sadie). What's the matter, you look low !

Sadie. Low ? Maybe. It's this rain, I guess.

O'Hara. You ought to try getting out for a walk.

Sadie. I was out this morning. I went to that half-caste family you told me about last night. I asked them if they wouldn't take me in to board. They closed the door in my face so fast you'd have thought I had smallpox.

O'Hara. Don't you care. You're better off here.

Sadie (*dryly*). I'm not so sure !

(*A moment's silence, save for the rain.*)

Listen to it. Don't it make you want to scream ? And when you do scream, what good does it do you ? You haven't got any strength left—you're hopeless—you're miserable !

O'Hara. That's no way to talk, Miss Sadie. Don't sound like you.

Sadie (*rising*). Forget it. I've got the fantods. I'll get over 'em— you see. (*She hesitates—moves a little* L. *below the table—then returns to* O'Hara.) I—I—I've just had a run in with that Davidson.

O'Hara (*moving to below the deck-chair*). Yeah ! What about ?

Sadie. He's not going to let me go to Apia—so he says. (*She pauses.*) And anybody can see with two glass eyes that this side of the Equator the reverend's in right and I'm in wrong. What I'm trying to figure out is what devil's trick he'll use to stop me.

O'Hara. I don't see what he can do.

SADIE.   Neither do I—but we don't say it with bells—either of us !
(*Pauses.*)   There's something about that crow that isn't human.
He's deep—he's creepy !   I guess it's his eyes—they look right into
you—seem to know what you're thinking.   Something tells me
I'm going to need friends soon, Handsome.   I'm far from home !

O'HARA.   Well, any time you call for help, I'm right here, don't
forget that, and if there's any help needed . . .

SADIE (*with a half smile*).   Thanks !   Thanks !

O'HARA.   Looka here,!   If something should go wrong—that
is, about your getting to Apia—what'll you do ?   You might as
well make plans.

SADIE.   What'll I do ?   That means you're afraid something will
go wrong ?

O'HARA.   No !   No !   But if the old nose-pusher gets around
the Governor somehow, and they do stop you somehow, what'll
you do ?

SADIE.   I don't know.

O'HARA.   Go back to the States, I suppose ?

SADIE.   No—no !   (*She gives a sudden movement of terror.*)
There's no way they can make me go back to the States, is there ?

O'HARA.   I don't see how, unless you want to !

(SADIE'S *eyes have suddenly become round and fixed as though a great
fear had seized her.   She sits* R. *of the table, gazing into space.
Suddenly she buries her head in her hands.*)

Why, what's the matter, Miss Sadie ?

SADIE (*through her teeth*).   I won't go back to the States.   They
couldn't make me go, could they ?

O'HARA.   You don't want to go to Honolulu either, I suppose ?

SADIE (*disgusted*).   No—no !

(*There is a pause.   She stares out before her.*)

O'HARA (*sitting on the* R. *corner of the table, above her*).   You
could go to Sidney.   Work's easy to get.   Living's cheap, they say.
I'd head that way instead of Apia if I were you.   There's a boat
twice a month.   That's where I'm bound as soon as I shed these hash
marks—that'll be one month and three days.

SADIE (*without turning*).   What are you going to do there ?

O'HARA.   Going into the building business.   Old shipmate of
mine has his own place and wants a partner—these three years Biff's
been at me to get my discharge and come in with him.   You'd like
this Biff.   We joined the service same time, sixteen years ago.

SADIE.   I'm glad you're fixed, Handsome, and you ought to do
fine !

O'HARA.   Then there's another thing.   If you go to Sidney
now, I'll be hoving in sight in a few weeks.   Not that that might
mean so much to you, maybe.

SADIE (*turning slowly in her chair and giving him a curious look*).
Mean so much ?   I haven't so many friends, Handsome, but what

I could do with one more. (*She smiles a strange, wistful, tender smile.*) You're an awful funny fellow, Handsome.

O'HARA. I guess I'm the dumbell king, all right.

SADIE (*thoughtfully, her chin in her hands*). I thought I knew most all there was to know about men, until you came along, but . . .

O'HARA (*after a pause*). How about it ?

SADIE. About what ?

O'HARA. Changing your route and going to Sidney anyway.

SADIE (*slowly*). Yes, why not ? (*She rises, and moves a pace* R.) I guess no one can stop me from doing that ! (*She swings round to face* O'HARA *with a laugh and seems to throw off her despondency.*) God ! What a poor simp I was to get the wind up all over nothing ! There was I jumping with the shakes and nervous as a witch just because that dismal crumb Davidson wouldn't let me go to Apia. (*Moving* L. *below the table.*) Well, Apia my foot—it's Sidney for mine !

(*A native appears at the verandah. He wears a raincoat of rushes over his lava lava and a dripping straw hat.*)

O'HARA (*crossing to the native*). What belong you want—lookum see.

NATIVE. I belong make fetch Governor's letter. (*He holds letter out to* O'HARA.)

O'HARA (*taking the letter and scanning the envelope, then moving towards* SADIE). It's—for you.

SADIE (*moving towards* O'HARA *and taking it gingerly*). For me—who's sending me a letter ? (*She looks at it, then at* O'HARA.) It's —it's from the Governor's office. (*She holds it fearfully; her hand trembling.*)

O'HARA (*turning to the native*). Sahulanua mi—make go.

(*The native exits.*)

(*To* SADIE.) Better open it.

(SADIE *opens the letter with nervous twistings. She reads it in silence.*)

SADIE (*having read letter, reads it aloud in a monotonous voice*). Listen to this !—" It has been brought to the attention of the Governor that your presence in Pago Pago is not best for the public good. An order of deportation has therefore been issued, in compliance with which you will leave this Island on the first boat. A passage from this port to San Francisco . . . (*her voice falters a second, but she goes on bravely*) . . . San Francisco, on the *S.S. Cumberland*, leaving Pago Pago on the 6th inst., will be procured for you, and a sufficient sum of money given you for the necessities of the journey.

" Signed, JOHN C. ROSS,
" *Secretary.*"

(*She stands motionless, mechanically refolding the letter with a vague
stare. Then, enraged with a growing sense of injustice.*) I won't go
back to 'Frisco—they can't make me. There's reasons I can't tell
you ! I've got some rights, haven't I . . . ? (*She stops, unable to
continue.*)

O'HARA (*soothingly*). Now don't get nervous. I tell you what.
Go see the Governor yourself right away. Ask him as a favour
to let you stay here until the Sidney boat goes. That'll only mean
three or four days more.
SADIE. Will he see me ?
O'HARA. Hurry up before he goes for dinner—it's only two
steps !
SADIE. All right, I'll make him listen ! He's got to listen !
O'HARA. Want me to go with you ?
SADIE. Wait till I get my hat.

(SADIE *rushes into her bedroom with a whirl of the bead curtains,
leaving* O'HARA *on the stage. He eases further* L. DAVIDSON
appears on the verandah and enters the room. A second later
SADIE, *slamming a hat on her head, reappears. She stops short on
seeing* DAVIDSON. *He gives no evidence of seeing her, but continues
across the room, as though to go upstairs. Her eyes flashing,*
SADIE *crosses up and intercepts him.*)

So you're back, are you ? You low down skunk, what have you
been saying—to the Governor about me ?
REV. DAVIDSON (*up* R.C., *in a quiet voice*). I've been hoping to
have another talk with you, Miss Thompson.
SADIE (*between her teeth*). You miserable snail snatcher. I
wouldn't talk with you, if you and me were the only people left on
earth. You're so doggone mean, it makes me sick even to look at
you. That's what I think of you, coming to me with all that guff
you spilled about salvation—then going and having me deported
on top of it—you low lived . . .
O'HARA. Sadie—for God's sake ! (*He goes up, to above the*
L. *end of the table, as if to check her.*)
REV. DAVIDSON. I am wholly indifferent to the abuse you think
fit to heap on me, Miss Thompson—but I am puzzled as to the
cause of it.
SADIE. You know what you've been and done—filling the
Governor up with a lot of filthy lies about me—and now this comes
—and I've got to beat it on the next boat. (*She crumples the
Governor's order in her fist, waving it at* DAVIDSON.)
REV. DAVIDSON. You could hardly expect him to let you stay
here under the circumstances.
SADIE (*screaming*). What did the Governor know or care about
me until you went and hauled your hooks into me ? It's you that
did it—you did it all !

REV. DAVIDSON. I don't want to deceive you, Miss Thompson. I urged the Governor to take the only steps consistent with his obligations.

SADIE. Why couldn't you let me be ? Was I doing you any harm—was I ?

REV. DAVIDSON. You may be sure if you had, I would be the last man to resent it.

SADIE. You don't think I *want* to stay in this rain hole, do you ?

REV. DAVIDSON (*smiling grimly*). In that case, I don't see what cause for complaint you have ! You are being given every opportunity of getting out. (*He makes for the stairs.*)

O'HARA (*moving up and pulling at* SADIE's *arm*). Sadie—Sadie—come on—don't talk any more.

SADIE (*shaking off* O'HARA *and following* DAVIDSON; *putting herself directly in front of him and shrieking, words tumbling pell-mell*). You ! You ! I know your kind, you dirty two-faced mutt ! I'll bet when you were a kid you caught flies and pulled their wings off —I bet you stuck pins in frogs, just to see 'em wiggle and flap while you read 'em a Sunday School lesson. I know you ! You'd tear the heart out of your grandmother if she didn't think your way and tell her you were saving her soul—you—you—you psalm-singing ——!—!—!

(*Her crazy words end in an inarticulate shriek of rage. During the above, as though drawn by* SADIE's *clamour,* MRS. DAVIDSON *runs down the stairs,* DR. *and* MRS. MACPHAIL *appear behind her;* HORN, *astonished out of his usual calm, enters from the store.* MRS. HORN *also peers through the door. They watch the finish of the scene between* SADIE *and* DAVIDSON *in fearful wonder. Following her outburst,* SADIE *breaks into sobs and is pulled out of the scene by* O'HARA.)

(SADIE *and* O'HARA *cross* R. *to the verandah noisily, and exit.*)

(*No word is spoken on the stage.* DAVIDSON *stands in terrible silence. His wife, her hands clasped, watches him.* HORN *signals his wife.* MRS. HORN *withdraws, followed by* HORN. *On the stage are the* MACPHAILS *and the* DAVIDSONS *only.*)

MRS. DAVIDSON. Alfred—this sort of thing must stop. It can't go on—it's wearing you out. That woman is possessed of devils.

REV. DAVIDSON. Yes—she is possessed of devils. (*In a deliberate voice.*) However, you will be glad to hear that the Governor has acted at last. Miss Thompson will leave on the first boat that goes.

(MRS. MACPHAIL, *followed by the* DOCTOR, *moves down,* L. *of the table.*)

DR. MACPHAIL (*wearily*). How soon will that be ?

REV. DAVIDSON. The San Francisco boat is due here from Sidney next Tuesday. She's to sail on that.

DR. MACPHAIL (*with a sigh*). Four days more !

REV. DAVIDSON (*looking at his watch*). It's half past six. (*To* MRS. DAVIDSON.) Are you ready, Hester ? (*He goes to the stairs slowly.*)

MRS. DAVIDSON. Yes, Alfred.

(DAVIDSON *mounts the stairs and exits.*)

(*To* MRS. MACPHAIL.) No matter where we are, always we make it a point to read a chapter of the Gospel either after tea or before retiring for the night. Then we study it with the commentaries and discuss it thoroughly. It's a great training for the mind.

(MRS. DAVIDSON *mounts the stairs and exits.*)

(*The* MACPHAILS *exchange glances.* DR. MACPHAIL *drags on his pipe and turns to his wife.*)

DR. MACPHAIL. That settles Miss Thompson's hash, I guess. (*He moves* R., *above the table.*)

MRS. MACPHAIL (*sighing*). These incessant scenes are very trying. I don't understand them. They horrify me. (*She sits above the table and opens her needlework bag.*)

DR. MACPHAIL (*by the deck-chair,* R.C., *puffing*). Um-m—But who's to blame ? Even a rabbit, you know, tears at the trap closing over it. (*He sits in the deck-chair.*)

(MRS. MACPHAIL *sighs and stitches on her comforter. Somewhere from above there comes a voice lifted in prayer. It reverberates above the steady downpour of the rain.* MACPHAIL *gestures to his wife. His finger is at his lips. She nods.*)

MRS. MACPHAIL. Yes ! I heard him last night. The partition between the room is so thin. I thought he'd never stop.

DR. MACPHAIL. I suppose he's praying for the soul of Sadie Thompson.

MRS. MACPHAIL. No wonder Mrs. Davidson looks like a ghost. She's so sensitive to sin. She tells me she hasn't closed her eyes since we came, thinking of that unmentionable woman under the same roof with her.

DR. MACPHAIL. Hm ! The founder of her religion wasn't so squeamish.

MRS. MACPHAIL. Don't joke about such things please, Robert.

(*She bites her thread in virtuous, wifely reproof.* SADIE *and* O'HARA *are now seen entering the verandah.* O'HARA *is half supporting* SADIE, *who, on seeing that the room is occupied by* DR. *and* MRS. MACPHAIL, *sinks into a chair by the verandah rail.* O'HARA *enters the room and crosses to* L. *of* MACPHAIL.)

O'HARA (*in a low voice*). Excuse me, Doctor—but—Miss Thompson isn't feeling well. Will you see her for a moment ?

DR. MACPHAIL (*rising*). Certainly.

O'Hara. She's right out there. I'll bring her in. (*He eases* R., *and beckons to* Sadie.) Sadie, here's Doctor MacPhail. Tell him what you want.

(Sadie *enters.* O'Hara *moves towards her and speaks in a lower voice.*)

I've got to get back for inspection now. I'll come around later. See you later—now keep your chin up.

(*They shake hands.*)

(O'Hara *exits quickly at the verandah.*)

(Sadie *crosses slowly to* Dr. MacPhail, *who sets the chair for her* R. *of the table.* Sadie *sits, looking nervously at* Mrs. MacPhail.)

Dr. MacPhail. This is my wife—Miss Thompson.

(Mrs. MacPhail *glances quickly at her husband, who pantomimes her to be pleasant.* Sadie *nods;* Mrs. MacPhail *does likewise.*)

Mrs. MacPhail (*nervously gracious*). I—I—believe we are fellow lodgers.

Sadie (*apathetically*). Yes.

(*There is an embarrassed pause.* MacPhail *signals for his wife to go.*)

Mrs. MacPhail (*rising*). Has the rain lessened at all ?

Sadie. No-o—not much.

Mrs. MacPhail (*crossing above the table to the verandah*). Last night there was a tiny bit of sunset shining through from somewhere —perhaps there is tonight. I'm going to see.

(Mrs. MacPhail *exits* R., *with nervous flutterings.*)

Dr. MacPhail. Sorry to hear you're not feeling well.

Sadie (*tensely*). Oh, I'm well enough—not really sick. O'Hara said that because I just had to see you. (*She clasps her hands until the knuckles show white.*)

Dr. MacPhail (*gently, as he moves to the deck-chair and sits*). Yes, Miss Thompson ?

Sadie. It's this, doctor ! I've been ordered to clear out of here on a boat that's going to San Francisco.

Dr. MacPhail. So I understand.

Sadie (*hoarsely*). Well, it isn't convenient for me to go back to San Francisco now. I've just been to see the Governor about it. He didn't want to speak to me, I'll say, but I wouldn't let him shake me off. Finally he said he had no objection to my staying here until the next boat to Sidney goes, if the Reverend Davidson would stand for it.

Dr. MacPhail (*dubiously*). I don't know exactly what I can do.

Sadie (*desperately*). Well I thought maybe you wouldn't mind asking the Reverend Davidson if he'd let me go to Sidney instead. I swear to go ; I won't start anything here—if he'll only let me stay. I won't go out of my room if that will suit him. It's only three or four days longer.

DR. MACPHAIL (*touched by her apparent desperation*). I'll ask him.

SADIE. Tell him I can get work in Sidney—straight stuff. (*Rising.*) It isn't asking much. I know I've talked to him awful—but he got me so mad. But I'll admit he's got me beat now. Tell him I just can't go back to San Francisco—there's reasons—I just can't ! (*She goes to the deck-chair and catches* MACPHAIL'S *hand in hers.*) Please—please !

DR. MACPHAIL. When I see him I'll do what I can. (*He rises.*)

SADIE (*inarticulately*). Thank you—thank you !

(MACPHAIL *turns up towards the verandah as though to follow his wife.* SADIE *sees he is not going to do it immediately. She goes after him.*)

Oh—couldn't you do it now ? I can't settle to a thing until I know the dope one way or another.

DR. MACPHAIL. Oh well, all right.

(*He crosses up reluctantly and mounts the stairs.* SADIE *crosses after him and listens.*)

DR. MACPHAIL (*calling*). Oh, Davidson !

REV. DAVIDSON (*heard off, upstairs*). What is it Doctor ?

DR. MACPHAIL. I want to speak to you about something. Shall I come up ?

REV. DAVIDSON. No, I'll come right down !

(*During the above* SADIE *stands by the staircase listening tensely. On hearing this she scurries down* L. *towards her doorway.* DR. MACPHAIL *descends.*)

SADIE (*moving up and frantically tugging at* MACPHAIL'S *arm*). Tell him I ask his pardon—tell him I'm sorry.

DR. MACPHAIL. Yes—yes ! Better get into your room, Miss Thompson.

(*He motions her to go into her room.* DAVIDSON *is heard descending.* SADIE *hurries to obey.* DAVIDSON *appears and descends. A flicker comes into his eye as he notices that the bead curtain into* SADIE'S *room is still moving.*)

REV. DAVIDSON (*coolly*). Well, Doctor, what can I do for you ? (*He comes to above the table.*)

DR. MACPHAIL (L. *of the table*). It's—er—it's about Miss Thompson.

(DAVIDSON *stands frigidly waiting for* MACPHAIL *to continue.*)

The Governor has told her that if you have no objection he will allow her to remain here until she can take the boat for Sydney.

Rev. Davidson. I'm sorry, Dr. MacPhail, but it is useless to discuss the matter.

Dr. MacPhail. It appears the girl has reasons for not wanting to return to San Francisco. I don't see that it makes any difference if she goes to Sydney instead. It's only a matter of a few days.

Rev. Davidson (*slowly*). Why is she unwilling to go back to San Francisco ?

Dr. MacPhail. I didn't enquire—and I think one does better to mind one's own business.

Rev. Davidson. You mean this interference for the best, Doctor, but my mind is made up.

Dr. MacPhail (*very slowly; moving to* Davidson). If you want to know what I think—I think you are harsh and tyrannical.

Rev. Davidson (*with a gentle smile*). I'm terribly sorry you should think that of me, Dr. MacPhail. (*Easing* r. *of the table and turning there.*) Believe me, my heart bleeds for that unfortunate woman— but I cannot find it in my conscience to change the decision. If the Governor wishes to do so on his own account, that is his business.

Dr. MacPhail. He won't—and you know why. (*A long look passes between the two.*)

Rev. Davidson (*with a melancholy smile*). Please don't bear malice toward me because I cannot accede to your wish. I respect you very much, Doctor, and I should be sorry if you thought ill of me.

Dr. MacPhail (*coldly*). I have no doubt you have a sufficiently good opinion of yourself to bear mine with equanimity.

Rev. Davidson (*with a gloomy chuckle*). That's one on me !

(Davidson *turns and exits upstairs.*)

(Sadie's *door opens fearfully. She comes out. A pause.*)

Dr. MacPhail (*averting his eyes from hers.*) I'm sorry.

(*He shakes his head. A sob breaks from* Sadie. *She covers her face and stands shaking before him.*)

Sadie. Oh !—Oh !—Oh !

Dr. MacPhail (*in sudden pity*). Don't give up hope. I think it is a shame the way they're treating you. I'll go and see the Governor myself.

Sadie (*brokenly*). Will you ? Will you ? Now ?

Dr. MacPhail (*going toward the verandah*). Now !

Sadie (*inarticulately*). You're awful good—awful good !

(Mrs. MacPhail *enters from the verandah.*)

Mrs. MacPhail. Where are you going, Robert ?

Dr. MacPhail (*at* r.c., *curtly*). Just a step. I'll be back in two minutes.

Mrs. MacPhail. Dinner's nearly ready.

(Sadie *shudders and sobs.*)

DR. MACPHAIL (*turning to look at her*). Don't cry, Miss Thompson—I think I can do something.

SADIE (*struggling for composure*). God bless you—Doctor—God bless you—you don't know what this means to me.

(MACPHAIL *exits*.)

(SADIE *sinks into the chair* L. *of the table.* MRS. MACPHAIL *is evidently deeply curious but she says nothing; she unrolls her sewing, sitting* R. *of the table.* SADIE *sits in stony silence, twisting her hands drearily.*)

MRS. MACPHAIL (*attempting to be charitable*). Everything is so damp, my needle has rusted in just these few minutes.

SADIE (*in a desolate voice*). Yes—even your bones would rust around here.

(*The silence is punctured by the rain.*)

(*Off* L. *we hear the clatter of* MRS. HORN *and the children.* MRS. HORN *enters with more dishes. She waddles to the table.*)

MRS. HORN (*to* MRS. MACPHAIL). Dinner very soon happen !— mebbe five, mebbe ten minutes now—better you make ready. (*She sets the dishes down noisily.*)

(HORN *enters up* L., *from the store.*)

HORN (*crossing* R., *above the table*). The din of my spouse, and the spluttering of Hamburg steak—not to mention the odour of indifferent grease—have detached me from my slumbers. (*He sprawls into his cane chair and continues in elaborate mockery as he sniffs.*) I detect our menu ! The hamburg steak of our luxurious table d'hote you are surely familiar with by this time, Mrs. MacPhail. As a flanking dish we offer you fried bananas, I believe. My fair Ameena, here, rarely varies the diet—she has deduced that it is substantial, satisfying and easy to prepare. She is a wise woman —she knows that ten minutes after consummation it won't matter whether one has dined on truffled grouse or hamburg steak, so why bother. Isn't that so, my beloved ?

(*Arms akimbo, nodding with pride,* MRS. HORN *listens to this oration. She smiles a vast, beaming smile.*)

MRS. HORN (*proudly*). That man—my husband—he talk damn fine—what ? (*Wisely.*) Hui !—That's right—That's, right.

HORN. See ! She concurs ! No more need be said.

MRS. MACPHAIL (*for the purpose of making conversation*). At that I quite agree with you, Mr. Horn. Most of us think too much about our stomachs. Take Mr. Davidson, he scarcely eats anything —but he is a very strong man—unusually strong—

(*Nodding wisely, her head cocked to one side,* MRS. HORN *listens to the above. Now she breaks in excitedly.*)

Mrs. Horn. Muihichia ! Me tell you something. Meestaire Davidson belong damn big Ju-ju-ija !

Horn (*pretending reproof*). My dear Ameena !

Mrs. Horn. All I same I know ! He Ju-ju-ija !

Mrs. MacPhail (*biting her thread*). What *is* she saying ?

Horn (*with amused mockery*). My wife in her gentle Polynesian way is tendering a high compliment to the Reverend Davidson—she says Mr. Davidson reminds her of a Ju-ju-ija !

Mrs. MacPhail. Whatever does she mean ?

Horn. My knowledge of the Ju-ju-ija is limited. When we got civilized here most of the Ju-ju-ijas packed off to remote places to weave their spells in peace. (*He turns to* Mrs. Horn.) He ate up devils, didn't he, Ameena ?

Mrs. Horn. Yes—Yes—Ju-ju-ija he ate plenty devil—know everything—see everything—my father's time, plenty Ju-ju-ija—now all gone !

(*She exits into the store.*)

Horn. A species of wizard, you perceive ! (*He smiles maliciously.*) Knew everything ! Saw everything ! Lived by the power of thought! A grilled goat chop had no charms for him. When hungry he simply ferreted out a devil and ate him up for tea.

Sadie (*jumping to her feet*). God ! It gives me the willies to hear that kind of talk.

(Sadie *crosses* R. *nervously toward the verandah, looking out in the direction of the Governor's house. While her back is turned,* Horn *and* Mrs. MacPhail *exchange glances, pregnant with meaning. The rain beats down pitilessly. In the silence we hear again the rumble of* Davidson's *voice, coming from above. He is praying.* Sadie, *returning, begins to shiver. She shakes so that it is noticeable to* Mrs. MacPhail. *Reaching the table, she takes a glass of water and tries to drink. The glass drops from her trembling hand and crashes to the floor.*)

Sadie (*shaking*). Oh ! I'm sorry—I'm sorry !

Mrs. MacPhail (*half rising*). You are ill, Miss Thompson.

Sadie (*moving away to* R.C.). No—I'm all right—this rain chills you—don't it ?

Horn (*producing his bottle*). Here—drink this.

Sadie (*taking the bottle*). Thanks ! (*She gulps the drink, returns the bottle to* Horn *and asks in a hushed voice.*) That's Reverend Davidson upstairs, isn't it ?

Horn. Sounds like his voice.

Sadie. Give me another—please.

(Horn *hands her the bottle. She gulps it.*)

What's he saying ?

(*She jerks her head in the direction of upstairs. We hear* Davidson's *voice saying* " Amen." *The praying finishes.*)

HORN (*ironically*). He said " Amen ! "

SADIE. Either I'm jinxed or this stuff is, Horn. I can't seem to feel it ! Maybe your wife's Juijua is after me ! (*She laughs a little crazily.*) What's that the old jig does ? Sees everything—knows everything ? (*She drinks again.*) Well, that's the kind of eye the Reverend Davidson has, all right ! He'd look right into you and know what you were trying to hide. It wouldn't be any use to try to keep much from him, would it ? (*She gives the bottle to* HORN.)

(*A* NATIVE GIRL *enters with an old cow bell, which she rings vigorously, announcing dinner.* MRS. HORN *follows with two steaming platters.* HORN *rises lazily.*)

HORN. Ha, the feast is served !

MRS. MACPHAIL (*rising, crossing to* L. *of the table, and sitting there*). For myself, I doubt whether I can eat a bite.

(MRS. DAVIDSON *is seen descending the stairs.* SADIE *sees her coming, pauses irresolutely, undecided what to do. Then she turns and walks quickly off via the verandah.* MRS. DAVIDSON *makes no comment on* SADIE'S *flight. She takes her place* L. *of the table in silence.* MRS. HORN *gives orders to the native girl and they exit up* L.)

(DAVIDSON *appears and begins to descend. As he comes into the room he notes that* MACPHAIL *is absent.*)

REV. DAVIDSON (*amiably, to* MRS. MACPHAIL). Isn't your husband dining ?

MRS. MACPHAIL (*nervously*). He just stepped out for a minute.

REV. DAVIDSON (*with a peculiar smile*). Where has he gone ?

MRS. MACPHAIL. I couldn't say exactly.

REV. DAVIDSON (*almost amused*). Ah ! I think I can guess !

(*He seats himself above the table and bows his head. The others follow suit. There is a second's silence while grace is said.*)

(MACPHAIL *and* SADIE *appear on the verandah. The change in* SADIE *is extraordinary. Her hair is dishevelled and her eyes glare with fear. The tears stream down her face.* MACPHAIL *is silent and depressed. The two stand waiting patiently until grace is over.*)

REV. DAVIDSON (*lifting his head and seeing* SADIE ; *speaking in a pleasnt cordial voice*). Can I do something for you, Miss Thompson ?

(MACPHAIL *moves down* R. *of the deck-chair.*)

(SADIE *comes toward* DAVIDSON *with a horrible cringing movement. She checks at up* R.C.)

SADIE. I'm sorry for what I said to you today. For everything that's happened—I ask pardon.

Rev. Davidson (*smiling*). I guess my back's broad enough to bear a few hard words.

Sadie. You've got me beat, I'm all in. For God's sake don't make me go to 'Frisco. I'll go anywhere else you say.

(Davidson's *genial manner vanishes and his voice grows hard and stern. He leaves the table and comes to her.*)

Rev. Davidson. Why don't you want to go back there ?

Sadie (*craftily*). It's this way, Reverend Davidson. I'm trying to go straight now. If I go back to San Francisco I can't go straight.

Rev. Davidson. What will prevent you from going straight— if you really want to ?

Sadie. There's a man in San Francisco, who won't let me.

Rev. Davidson. Who is this man ?

Sadie (*at random*). Sort of politician. He's a bad man. I'm scared of him.

Rev. Davidson. San Francisco is a big place. It should not be difficult to keep out of his way—if you want to.

Sadie (*wildly*). He'll know, though—He'll know ! All the boats coming in are being watched.

Rev. Davidson. Do you mean to tell me that every boat coming into the port will be watched, on the chance you are on it !

Sadie. Yes—Yes !

Rev. Davidson (*in a terrible voice*). Come, Miss Thompson, these evasions are getting you nowhere. Why are you afraid to return to San Francisco ?

Sadie. I've told you. I can't go straight there.

Rev. Davidson (*rising and towering over* Sadie, *who puts her hands up to her face and cringes*). Shall I tell you why you are afraid to go back ?

Mrs. MacPhail (*to* Mrs. Davidson). I think you and I had better leave !

(Mrs. Davidson *nods and the two ladies rise, move up, and exit upstairs.*)

(Horn *taps* MacPhail *on the shoulder and the two men sneak off via the verandah.*)

(Sadie *and* Davidson *are now alone.* Sadie *cowers before him.*)

Rev. Davidson. You have told me lies. Now I shall tell you the truth. This politician you fear is a politician in uniform—and he wears a badge ! (*He takes her by the shoulders and his great shining eyes seem to bore into her soul.*) What you fear is—the penitentiary.

(Sadie *gives a sudden cry, then weakens at the knees and falls, clasping his legs.*)

Sadie. Don't send me back there. I swear to you before God, I'll be a good woman. I'll give all this up.

(DAVIDSON *leans over her, lifts her face, forces her to look at him.*)

DAVIDSON. Is that it—the penitentiary ?

SADIE (*faintly*). I was framed ! But I got away before they caught me. They'll nab me the moment I step off the ship, and it's three years for mine—three years—three years.

(DAVIDSON *lets go of* SADIE *and she falls in a heap on the floor, sobbing bitterly.*)

(*After a second, between her sobs.*) Give me a chance—one chance.

REV. DAVIDSON (*with shining eyes*). I'm going to give you the finest chance you've ever had.

SADIE (*taking hope, half rising*). I don't have to go back, you mean ?

REV. DAVIDSON. Yes, you'll have to go back. You will sail for San Francisco on Tuesday, as the Governor has ordered.

(SADIE *gives a groan of horror, sinks on the floor again and bursts into low, hoarse moans, scarcely human.*)

If you are truly repentant you will gladly accept this punishment. You will offer it to God as the atonement for your sins. (*The missionary's lips move silently in prayer. Then, gently.*) When you want me, Sadie Thompson, call for me—I will come.

(DAVIDSON *is extraordinarily moved. Tears run down his cheeks.*)

At any hour—day or night—when you need me I will come. I shall be waiting for your call.

(*He turns and slowly starts toward the stair.* SADIE'S *shuddering moans become fainter. They are now deep, tortured sighs.* DAVIDSON *begins to mount the stairs.* SADIE *rouses herself. She gives a little cry.* DAVIDSON *pauses.*)

SADIE (*struggling to her feet*). Reverend Davidson—wait a minute! (*A flicker of craft comes into* SADIE'S *eyes—the craft of desperation. Her expression indicates that her mind is working rapidly. She crosses up* C., *below the banisters and clasps her hands.*) Reverend Davidson—you're right. I am a bad woman, but I want to be good, only I don't know how. So you let me stay here with you, then you can tell me what to do, and no matter what it is I'm going to do it for you.

REV. DAVIDSON (*looking down on her, shaking his head*). No, you can't stay here. You've got to go back to San Francisco ; you've got to serve your time.

SADIE (*looking at him astonished after her offer*). You mean to say, if I repent and I want to be good—I still have to go to the penitentiary ? (*Clutching the banisters, throwing her last plea.*) But I was framed, I tell you ! I was framed !

REV. DAVIDSON. Innocent or guilty, you must serve your sentence ! It's the only way you can prove to God that you are worthy of His mercy.

SADIE.   Innocent or guilty ? What kind of a God are you talking about ?   Where's your mercy ?   Ah, no, REVEREND Davidson, I guess that repentance stuff is off. (*She turns away, moving down* R.C.)

REV. DAVIDSON.   Was it ever on, Miss Thompson ?

SADIE (*turning to face the stairs*). Whether it was or not, it's off now ! The way you figure out God, He's nothing but a Cop.

REV. DAVIDSON.   You've got to go back to San Francisco !

SADIE (*throwing discretion to the winds*). Straight orders from your private heaven, eh ? Ah, no, REVEREND Davidson, your God and me could never be shipmates, and the next time you talk to Him (*she steps up a pace or two and shouts in his face*) you tell Him this for me : Sadie Thompson is on her way to Hell !

REV. DAVIDSON (*drawing himself up to full height and shouting back at her*). Stop ! This has gone far enough !

SADIE (*in wild hysteria*). No ! It hasn't gone far enough ! You've been telling me what's wrong with me. Now I'll tell you what's wrong with you. You keep yelling at me—be punished ! Go back and suffer ! (*Turning down* R.C.) How do you know what I have suffered ? You don't know, you don't care : you don't even ask, and you call yourself a Christian (*turning to face him*). You're nothing but a miserable witch burner—that's what you are—you believe in torture. You know you're bit and you're strong and you've got the law on your side—and the power to hang me. All right ! But I want to tell you this : I've got the power to stand here and say to you—Hang me and be damned to you !

(*She stampedes* L. *and into her room, sobbing hoarsely.*)

DAVIDSON'S *lips move in prayer as*

the CURTAIN *falls.*

ACT III

SCENE 1

The SCENE *is the same as the preceding. It is night; four days later.*

The rain is beating persistently on the roof. On the verandah the shades are drawn. Indoors, the centre lamp is lit, casting a circle of reddish light on the floor below. The chairs above the table are pushed in. The corners of the room are heavily in shadow. Blending with the sound of the rain, as from a distance, we hear the ominous beating of festival drums.

As the CURTAIN *rises,* HORN *and his wife are alone on the stage.* HORN *is seated on the deck-chair under the lamp, reading.* MRS. HORN *is snoozing in the chair* L. *of the table, her head nodding, a palm-leaf fan slipping from her fingers.*

HORN (*reading aloud from his book*). Everything goeth—everything returneth—eternally rolleth the wheel of existence ! Everything dieth—everything blossometh forth again. Eternally runneth on the year of existence ! Thus spake Zarathustra ! (*He smacks his lips as though enjoying the sonorous rolling of the words.*) Good old Nietzsche !

(*There comes a faint cry from* SADIE'S *room—the cry of a person awakening from an uneasy sleep.*)

SADIE (*calling from her room*). Reverend Davidson ! Reverend Davidson !

(HORN *lays aside his book, and* MRS. HORN *opens one eye.*)

MRS. HORN. Ohm ! (*She struggles into an upright position and listens.*) She wake up ! Mebbe I go look-see, what ?

HORN (*wearily*). No ! Don't do anything. If God is good she is only turning over !

MRS. HORN (*sleepily*). Alumen—ta—mih—bah ! Tomorrow she go ! Trouble all finish, zazut !

HORN. Tomorrow she goes ! That episode endeth !

(*They both listen. The sound from* SADIE'S *room is repeated.* MRS. HORN *rises and crosses to the* L. *door, opening it gently.* SADIE'S *voice is heard.*)

SADIE (*crying from her room*). Reverend Davidson ! Reverend Davidson !

MRS. HORN (*at door*). He soon be coming. He soon be coming.

SADIE (*her voice is like a child's*). Hasn't he got back yet ?

MRS. HORN (*consolingly*). He come soon now. You go sleep !

SADIE. Oh—dear !

MRS. HORN. You good girl now—nothing be 'fraid . . .

62

(MRS. HORN *closes the door and returns to her chair. She rocks and* HORN *reads. There is a moment's silence. Then a loud knock is heard, seeming to come from the store.* MRS. HORN *starts.* HORN *sits erect and listens. The knock is repeated.*)

HORN.　Who in creation's that ?
MRS. HORN.　Mamut ! Mamut ! Who ?
HORN.　Go see, Ameena !
MRS. HORN (*fearfully*).　Me no like go ! Too many bad things happen.
HORN.　Damn !

(*He rises lazily, crosses* L., *and opens the store door.* O'HARA *enters.*)

Oh, it's you, is it ? Why the back way ?
O'HARA.　Nix—will you. (*He holds up a warning hand.*)
HORN (*returning to* R. *of the table*).　Where you been all week ?
O'HARA (*grimly, as he moves down to above the table*).　In the brig.
HORN (*with a smile*).　Yep ! I heard you was demi-tassing in the guard house.
O'HARA (*angrily*).　I'm out tonight, all right, though, they'll all find out.
HORN.　About time you come around. (*He sits,* R. *of the table.*) Nice doing we've been having.
O'HARA.　I'll bet you have ! (*Sitting on the upper edge of the table.*) Where's all your swell company ?
HORN.　Whole caboodle's gone over to that native witch dance on Tangu Island.
O'HARA (*bitterly*).　I had a hunch they'd go there. The Reverend couldn't pass up a chance like that, to get a few words in. Bet he busts the show up when the dancing starts.
HORN.　Yeah. He'll be needing new brands to snatch from the burning now he's nipped poor Sadie Thompson out of the flames.
O'HARA.　He can't get back before midnight, anyway—so we've got happy moments for a couple of hours. (O'HARA *pauses, then says in a different voice, pointing to* SADIE'S *room.*) How is she ?
HORN (*shaking his head.*)　Not so good.
O'HARA.　What's he been doing to her ?
HORN.　Praying.
O'HARA.　Praying ?
HORN.　Praying !
O'HARA.　Got her beached with his psalm stuff—what ?
HORN.　Beached and delirious, I'd say.
O'HARA (*standing*).　He took damn good care to get me stowed away before he started, didn't he ? Well, I beat him to it tonight.
HORN.　How did you get out ?
O'HARA (*with a short laugh, crossing* R.).　Walked out through the mess window. Little Griggs and Hodgson helped me—good boys, both of them—they ought to be here any minute now. (*He moves down* L. *of the deck-chair.*)

HORN. Um ! What's a-doing, O'Hara ? You arouse my curiosity.

O'HARA. If I was you, I'd ease off to bed with my old lady— and not have any curiosity.

HORN. You would, would you—and why would you do that ?

O'HARA (*winking*). I'd do that so's I wouldn't get blamed for anything, in case anything happened.

(HORN *gestures to his wife to leave them alone, in obedience to which she rises and waddles off into the store.*)

HORN (*with mock mournfulness*). Sounds like another row is starting ! Most unlucky day of my life—that day the *Orduna* came into port. (*He pauses, then goes on with elaborate mournfulness.*) I like my comfort ! For five days now this whole household has centred on that tormented Thompson girl in there while Davidson and Old Nick wrestled for her soul ! It's got me nervous !

O'HARA (*shortly*). Cheer up. It won't centre round her much longer ! What's she doing now—sleeping ?

HORN. I haven't heard her yell for Davidson for at least ten minutes, so let's hope so.

O'HARA (*sharply*). Get her out for me ! I'll tend to the rest of this.

HORN (*rising*). Gladly, gladly. My mind's a blank save for one fact—tomorrow Miss Sadie Thompson'll be on the high seas. (*He crosses below the table to* SADIE'S *door.*)

O'HARA (*grimly*). You'll bet she'll be !

HORN (*rapping on* SADIE'S *door*). Are you asleep, Miss Thompson ?

(*An inarticulate sound from* SADIE'S *room.*)

This is Horn. Will you come out a moment ? You're wanted.

SADIE (*listlessly*). All right.

(HORN, *with a shrug of relief, exits up* L. *hastily with a backward look at* O'HARA *of mingled mirth and pity.*)

(SADIE'S *door slowly opens. She stands there, her hand over her eyes, like a person waked from sleep. Her hair is uncurled and hangs straight about her shoulders and down her back. She wears an old white dressing-gown of towelling. Over her shoulders is thrown a knitted shawl. She stands vaguely, uncertainly, in her doorway. Her feet are thrust into bedroom slippers. Her eyes are tragic and dark-ringed, her face ghastly. The ghost of a smile comes to her mouth as she sees* O'HARA.)

O'HARA (*shocked at her appearance*). Sadie ! (*moving towards her.*) You look awful sick.

SADIE (*moving in a little*). I was wondering whether I'd see you before I left. You've been awful kind to me. I'll never forget it. I want to thank you.

O'HARA (*shortly; moving to her,* L. *of the table*). Look here,

Sadie—how long'll it take you to get packed ?

SADIE. I'm pretty well packed up now. Mrs. Horn helped me get ready after dinner.

O'HARA. That's good. Griggs and Hodgson'll be along any minute now, they're to tote your bags. You hurry up now and get dressed as fast as you can.

SADIE. Get dressed ?

O'HARA. You're leaving this place tonight.

SADIE. But the boat don't get in until tomorrow morning.

O'HARA. Your boat's going out tonight—and I'm going to see you get aboard her.

SADIE (*crossing him to* R. *of the table*). But I must wait for Mr. Davidson. He was going to see me on board. I . . .

O'HARA. Mr. Davidson isn't going to see you off.

SADIE (*getting frightened*). He isn't going to see me on board? What's happened ? Where is he ? (*She sinks into the chair* R. *of the table*.)

O'HARA (*moving up to above the table*). You're not going back to San Francisco—that's what's happened. You're leaving in a few minutes for the Samarkind Islands on a junk. You're going to wait there until the Sydney boat comes along. Then you're going to Sydney.

SADIE. Did Mr. Davidson say so ?

O'HARA (*moving to above the* R. *end of the table*). I say so ! You didn't think I was going to stand by and do nothing while they railroaded you back somewhere you didn't want to go, did you.

(SADIE *does not answer.* O'HARA *continues rapidly.*)

Hurry up, now, and get your clothes on. We've got time but none to spill.

(SADIE *still does not rise. She stares at* O'HARA *in a distracted way.* O'HARA *continues gently.*)

Now don't get scared—it's all fixed. You're going as far as the Samarkinds on a ginseng junk and all you'll have to do is to lie low there for a few days until the Sundey boat comes along.

SADIE (*hazily; her hand at her head*). What do you suppose Reverend Davidson would think if he came back and found me gone ?

O'HARA. Huh ! You know the old shouter better than I do. (*Chuckles.*) But I don't mind admitting that a sight of his face at that moment would slip me considerable quiet fun.

(*He pauses. She does not respond to his chuckle. He looks at her tenderly.*)

You've had a pretty bad time, I guess, these last few days. Just forget 'em. From now on everything's going to be fine. Just go put on a hat and dress, so's you'll be ready to start soon as the boys come.

C

Sadie. It's mighty sweet and fine of you to go to all this trouble for me.

O'Hara. Fine—fine nothing ! This ain't one small bit what I'd like to do for you—if I got the chance.

Sadie. Your doing this — it makes me kind of want to cry — but . . .

O'Hara. What's the but ?

Sadie. I can't do it.

O'Hara. Why can't you do it ?

Sadie. I'm going through with what I've got to go through with.

O'Hara (grimly). Are you afraid of Davidson ? He'll never get hold of you again. I'll see to that.

Sadie. No, no, that isn't it at all. It would be awful hard for me to make you understand what's come over me. I can't understand myself. (A look almost of ecstasy comes into her face.) Listen, Handsome ! That day—remember—it seems years ago—that day the Governor's letter came—I lost my nerve. I ran around like a chicken with its head cut off. I was all over sweat—and I thought— I thought, I'll see if I can't fool him—so I told him a lie as to why I didn't want to go back to San Francisco—but he saw right through me—he looked right into me—he knew—he knew. (She stops, then goes on rapidly, pantingly.) Seemed to me then a great net was catching me. I knew nothing was any use—but I tried again. I called him back. I told him I had been a bad woman and I wanted to repent. That was a lie. I'd figured out things long ago and I didn't think I was bad, so there wasn't anything to repent about. I'd doped it out that some folks have luck, some haven't—all folks can't be the same, anyway—who knows what's good or what's bad ? Nobody. So I let it go at that—and didn't think too much. I'm not saying, of course, there hadn't been tough moments when you had to think. (She clings to O'Hara's arm, shaken by memories.)

O'Hara. Sadie—Sadie—you're getting all upset. Please, baby, don't go on so.

Sadie (not heeding the interruption). Well, I told Davidson I'd repent. I thought maybe he'd be easier on me if he thought I'd fallen for his line. But he saw through that, too. Then I lost my head and talked to him terrible but he didn't mind. He followed me into my room and asked me if I would kneel down and pray, and I was so desperate that I said " Yes." Oh, Handsome ! He knelt down and began to pray. He prayed a long time—hours ! I didn't pay much attention at first. The rain was coming down straight and heavy. Outside, everything was damp and clammy. I kept wishing the mosquitoes would stop humming—I was kind of numb. There was some dreadful fear catching at me—but all at once I began to listen—sort of in spite of myself—Oh, Handsome . . . (Her voice breaks, she cannot go on.)

O'Hara (gently; moving round above and r. of her chair). Go on—go on—spill it all. (He pats her shoulder.)

Sadie. Mr. Davidson prayed and prayed—and all of a sudden

there was I out in a big, bright, beautiful place. Seemed to me all
my life I had been in a fog and hadn't known it. He prayed for
hours and hours. I was awful tired—but sort of happy. I knew
I could be saved if I wanted, and I did want to repent. I told Mr.
Davidson how I'd tried to fool him first about repenting—but he
said he'd known it all along. (*She pauses, then goes on excitedly.*)
Then it came, Handsome ! I *did* feel sorry for what I'd been—
there was nothing phony about it ! I saw myself just as I was.
Oh, God ! Oh, God ! (SADIE *begins to cry in nervous exhaustion.
Her tears are the tears of strain, weariness and tension; her sobs,
jerky and wretched.*)

O'HARA (*very gently*). Sadie—this thing don't make you happy.
You don't realize—it ain't yourself. You've got to forget Mr.
Davidson and come with me.

SADIE. No—No—I couldn't—I couldn't. You don't know what
you're saying.

O'HARA. They're not going to send you back there with no one
to take care of you . . .

SADIE (*putting her hands to her ears*). I won't listen—I won't
listen—stop !—stop !

O'HARA. What's to hinder you repenting in Sydney—just as well
as in San Francisco—if you've got to repent ?

SADIE. You don't understand. I've got to go back and be
punished for what I've been—there's no other way out. I've got to
serve my time—then God will forgive me. It's the sacrifice I've got
to offer up for the life I've led. Oh, if it would only begin at once.
It's this waiting for it to start, that's so bad—all these days and days
I'll be alone on the boat. I'm weak. I'm afraid. I'm dreadfully
afraid. You've got to be very strong, Handsome, to live at all.
(*Almost as if to herself.*) It will be much easier in the penitentiary.

O'HARA (*in a strange, shocked voice*). What's that you're saying ?
The penitentiary ?

SADIE (*with a curious smile*). When I get to San Francisco,
Handsome, I've got to go to the penitentiary for—three years.

O'HARA (*staring back; under his breath*). God !

SADIE. Reverend Davidson says it doesn't make any difference
whether I was innocent or guilty, of what they framed me for. He
says that is God's way of letting me square myself. He says I've
got to accept an unjust punishment by man as a sacrifice to God.

O'HARA. You just listen to me. Get into your room and throw
your clothes on as fast as you can. (*He pulls her from her chair.*)

SADIE. Let go of me—let go ! (*She frees herself ferociously;
turns on him angrily.*) Don't you dare do that again ! I want you
to go away. Do you hear ? Get right out !

O'HARA (*brokenly*). Sadie—Sadie !

SADIE (*wildly, going* R.). I mean it! Get right out! Go away—go away.

O'HARA. Sadie—listen—please . . .

SADIE (*frantically; turning at* R.) Don't you come near me. Go
away !

(*There is a sound on the verandah of the rain-shutters being pulled aside, and hushed voices.* SADIE *and* O'HARA *listen. Then* O'HARA *moves to up* R.C. GRIGGS *and* HODGSON *enter cautiously. The former carries a basket of ripe pineapples. On seeing the tensity of the situation between* O'HARA *and* SADIE *they pause irresolutely.*)

O'HARA (*in a firm low voice*). Here's the two high-school boys, Sadie—come to say good-bye to you. They're going to put your things aboard the junk for you. (*His voice is soothing; the voice one uses to a tired fretful child.*)

(*Suddenly* SADIE *begins to cry again; she sinks into the deck-chair* R., *and sobs violently and hoarsely.* O'HARA *motions to* GRIGGS *and* HODGSON *to get* SADIE'S *baggage. The lads nod, cross quietly* L., *and enter* SADIE'S *room.*)

O'HARA (*when they have disappeared*). Sadie . . . listen, Sadie . . .
SADIE. Reverend Davidson ! Reverend Davidson ! Why don't he come ? Why don't he come . . .?

(GRIGGS *comes out with an old carpet bag in one hand and a shawl bundle in the other. He crosses to* O'HARA *and sets them down on the floor.*)

GRIGGS (*to* O'HARA, *in a low voice*). Most of the stuff is tied up pretty good—but how about the gramophone ?
O'HARA. Never mind. I'll bring that.

(HODGSON *enters with several large nondescript parcels of bulging shape.* SADIE *turns and sees* GRIGGS *and* HODGSON *moving her luggage.*)

SADIE (*crying out*). Oh, what are they doing ? (*Moving towards the verandah.*) They mustn't. They mustn't. (*She gives a scream.*) Reverend Davidson ! Reverend Davidson !
O'HARA. Sadie ! Someone'll hear you ! Don't for God's sake !
SADIE (*turning to face them*). Go away—all of you. Go away ! Mr. Davidson !
O'HARA (*to* GRIGGS). See if there isn't a coat or something in there. That old peeler's got her tranced.

(GRIGGS *goes quickly into* SADIE'S *room.*)

(*To* HODGSON.) We're taking her whether she wants to go or not.

(GRIGGS *re-appears with a coat belonging to* SADIE *over his arm. He gives it to* O'HARA.)

SADIE. They're taking my things. They mustn't take my things ! (*Pleadingly.*) Go away, please. Please let me be. Oh, Handsome, why do you make it so hard for me ?

(GRIGGS *and* HODGSON *exit* R. *with* SADIE'S *things.*)

O'HARA (L. *of* SADIE; *feelingly*). Don't you know, Sadie ? You ain't yourself !

SADIE (*earnestly*). I am myself ! I am myself ! That's what I've been trying to tell you ! (*Easing* R.) Reverend Davidson's a holy man—the Spirit of God is in him. He's different from you and me. He has made me different. (*Turning slowly to* O'HARA.) I've been born all over again—don't you see, Handsome ?

O'HARA. Yes—I see, and I see something else. (*He moves toward her.*) Remember, I told you if you ever needed a friend, I'd be here. Well, you need a friend—right now.

SADIE. Reverend Davidson's my friend.

O'HARA. Now, Sadie, you've got to listen to me. (*He waves a hand toward the direction the boys have taken.*) Those boys are waiting for us out there in the boat. They are going to row you out to the junk. You're going on that to the Samarkind Islands and then you're going to wait there until the Sydney boat comes along. And then you're going to take that to Sydney.

SADIE (*wildly*). I'm going back to San Francisco !

O'HARA. You're not going to San Francisco, you're going to Sydney.

(SADIE *looks at* O'HARA *with a strange new fright.*)

Sadie ! Out there you've got your whole life before you. We'll go away, where this damn rain or anything else can't follow us. Just you and me—like Biff and Maggie—fifty-fifty. You'll be Mrs. Tim O'Hara. It's Sydney and us—the whole damn works against the penitentiary. And I'm taking you whether you want to go out or not !

(SADIE *struggles to resist, but pleading, coaxing, cajoling, he is slowly but surely urging her toward the verandah.*)

SADIE (*despairingly*). You mustn't—you mustn't ! I'm saved I tell you. You'll send me to Hell ! (*Her voice now fairly rings with fear.*) Reverend Davidson ! Reverend Davidson !

(*The tall form of* DAVIDSON *suddenly appears on the verandah. He casts his hat and umbrella on the porch floor and strides into the room.*)

REV. DAVIDSON. Here I am, Miss Thompson. It seems I got here just about in time.

(O'HARA *stops in his effort to get* SADIE *from the room and stares threatingly at* DAVIDSON. SADIE *is between them.*)

SADIE. Oh—oh !

(SADIE *slips from* O'HARA'S *suddenly relaxed arms. There is something awesome about* DAVIDSON'S *appearance. Although out of breath as from running, his movements now are slow and decisive and his voice when he speaks, sure and contained.*)

REV. DAVIDSON. It seems I got here just about in time, Miss Thompson. (*He pauses, looks at* O'HARA, *then back to* SADIE.)

All evening I had a peculiar feeling you were in danger. It was almost as though God were whispering in my ear to hurry back.

O'HARA (L. *of* SADIE). Sadie—Sadie—don't pay any attention to him.

REV. DAVIDSON (*turning to* O'HARA). I'm sorry for you, O'Hara. What you are trying to do is a serious offence.

O'HARA (*heedlessly*). What you're trying to do would make a hyena cry.

REV. DAVIDSON. You are trying to abduct Sadie Thompson. You have made an attempt to defeat the law. It's likely to go hard with you.

O'HARA. That's my look out. God, what kind of a man are you, anyway ! Picking on this poor kid here. Getting her so she's half-crazy. Sending her back to where she's got to go to prison. You're one choice specimen, Reverend Davidson. I'll say that for you. They don't make your kind every day !

REV. DAVIDSON. You are a reckless, headstrong man, O'Hara— you are given to loud language and strong drink. Your officers apparently have no control of you. You are breaking barracks now, and attempting a high-handed crime. You defy the authority of State and God. You cannot go on the way you're going—and I shall see to it that you do not !

O'Hara. Begging your pardon, might I ask what you think you're going to do about it ?

REV. DAVIDSON (*sternly*). Get back to your barracks as fast as you can, O'Hara. Report here to me tomorrow, after Miss Thompson has gone.

O'HARA. To you ? Where do you get these ideas, anyway ? What are you ? God's pet what-not ? Eh ? If it's good advice you want to ladle out—keep it ! Your bunk gives me an earache ! On such rare moments as I think, I think for myself.

REV. DAVIDSON. All this is not helping your case. Watch what you say.

O'HARA. I'm here to watch out that Sadie don't make a fool-break. You've got to do some settling with me before she does any sailing.

SADIE (*breaking in*). You're wrong ! I know what I'm doing. I'm sorry, Handsome, but I see clear.

O'HARA. See clear ! Why this old gadget's got you so it's like you're doped.

(*The rain diminishes.*)

SADIE (*crossing* O'HARA *slowly towards the table*). I see what you don't see—what's happened to me don't happen to everybody. I was nothing. I was nobody. Now I'm something. I'm somebody. (*Standing by the chair,* R. *of the table.*) Reverend Davidson's shown me ! I'd have gone through my whole life never knowing I was anything if it hadn't been for him. It's a wonderful thing to know you've been made of some account—the only thing I can't see is how it happened to me !

(The rain stops.)

O'HARA (*up* R.C., *hesitatingly*).   Is that the way it is, Sadie ?

SADIE.   That's the way it is.

O'HARA.   What do you want me to do ?

SADIE.   I don't want you to do anything, except just not say anything more.

O'HARA (*huskily*).   All right !   I'll tell the boys to bring your things back.   (*A pause.*)   If you and me never see each other again I want to say this :   I'll not forget you—ever.

SADIE (*inaudibly*).   Good-bye.

(O'HARA *exits* R. *by the verandah; ignoring* DAVIDSON.)

(SADIE *turns, to see* O'HARA *disappear, then faces front again.* DAVIDSON *moves to above the table, by the* L. *end of it.*)

SADIE (*turning up above the chair* R. *of the table*).   Don't blame O'Hara, Reverend Davidson—it was all my fault.

REV. DAVIDSON.   My poor child, it was not your fault.   Far down the beach I heard your cry for help.   I heard you call my name.   I left MacPhail to take care of the canoe and bring in the women.

SADIE.   O'Hara thought he was helping me.   He didn't understand.

REV. DAVIDSON.   You may be sure, Miss Thompson, I shall give him every chance before I act.

SADIE (*desperately*).   Reverend Davidson—O'Hara's an awful simple fellow.   He seems rough and all that, but I've met lots of men—and I've never known one so good, take it all through, as him.   Please don't do anything to him.   I just can't bear to think of him—suffering—and in trouble.   He wouldn't know what to do.   It's all right for *me*—it was coming to me—but I can't bear to think that I've brought anything on to O'Hara.

REV. DAVIDSON.   Can't you see that indirectly you are responsible for the finest thing that could happen to O'Hara.   He is to have his chance—just as you had yours !   (*He stops; his eyes glow.*)

SADIE (*hopefully*).   Can't—can't—what's coming to me do for both of us ?

REV. DAVIDSON (*shaking his head*).   No one can pay another's reckoning—each one must pay his own.

SADIE.   Yes   (*She pauses.*)   But—you told me—maybe I can't understand right yet—you told me Christ took the punishment for all of us—when they crucified Him.

REV. DAVIDSON (*as to a child; moving to her*).   Sadie—Christ saved the world for us, but each of us must bear his share of the cross—it wouldn't be fair to leave the whole weight on His shoulders would it ?

SADIE.   No—I suppose it wouldn't !   When you're here, everything is so clear !   Everything's all right—but when you're away, I'm afraid !   I get to thinking of how wicked I used to be—and

I just can't believe it's all forgiven. (*Crossing down and to* L., *below the table.*) The days aren't so bad—but the nights ! That's when I begin to think and wonder ! If they're bad now, what are they going to be when you can't come any more—when I'm all alone. (*She gives a shudder of fear and a low cry of utter woe, and sinks into the chair* L. *of the table.*)

REV. DAVIDSON (*moving to below her chair*). When you are alone, my strength will come to you through prayers, which will be always on my lips. Little by little you yourself will grow stronger, surer—and presently the time will come when sin and terror are powerless to penetrate the great love God has wrapped around you. Then will you be redeemed—the kingdom and the glory will be yours.

SADIE (*in ecstasy*). Yes—yes—when you talk to me like that—I'm not afraid. That old life I led don't seem to belong to me at all—it was someone else—it wasn't me. When I feel that way, Reverend Davidson, does that mean I'm redeemed ?

REV. DAVIDSON (*gently*). Yes, Sadie. In the last few days you have become very close and dear to God. He has tested you and found you true. Tonight he sent the devil to tempt you—but you thrust away the devil. Once your soul lay like a stagnant pool in the lowest pit of the deepest valley. Tonight it has been lifted up to the sun—stagnant no longer, but cleansed, glorified, as the rain of heaven !

SADIE (*shaking her head sadly*). I guess people don't get things when they're tired.

REV. DAVIDSON (*gently*). And tomorrow will be a very busy day. You'll need all your strength. Try to get some sleep now.

SADIE (*covering her face with her hands*). Tomorrow ! Oh ! (*She gives a little moan. Then she rises and crosses to her door.*) If I wake up tonight and get afraid, will you come and pray with me ?

REV. DAVIDSON (*moving down* L. *of the table*). When I hear you call—I will come !

SADIE (*parting her curtains*). Yes—I'm pretty tired—pretty tired.

(*She exits weakly into her room.*)

(DAVIDSON'S *lips move in prayer. There is a look of great ecstasy in his eyes. Footsteps are heard on the verandah.* DR. *and* MRS. MACPHAIL *and* MRS. DAVIDSON *enter and remove their straw waterproofs.*)

DR. MACPHAIL (*taking off his goloshes*). A disagreeable experience ! But now that the episode is closed, I want to make one final observation. If heaven were promised me if I could get there in a canoe, I know where I would really land ! (*He puts the umbrella in the barrel* R.)

MRS. DAVIDSON (*moving to up* C.). I hope you found nothing wrong, Alfred ?

REV. DAVIDSON (*turning and moving down* R.C.). No ! (*Exultantly.*) A great happiness has come to me tonight ! I have had proof that Sadie Thompson has been reborn ; that I have been privileged to bring a lost soul into the loving arms of Jesus ! Truly the marvels of the Lord are demonstrated in strange ways ! I should never have known this so surely if it had not been for another's attempted sin.

(*He stands below the deck-chair.* MRS. DAVIDSON *moves down on his* L. MRS. MACPHAIL *crosses to up* L.C. *and sits in the* L. *chair above the table.*)

DR. MACPHAIL (*dryly, moving across to join his wife*). Since this sin has worked a benefit, isn't it a bit unkind to call it sin ?

REV. DAVIDSON (*turning; in a pleasant voice*). It seems to me, Doctor, you rather enjoy refusing to understand me. (*He sits in the deck-chair.*)

DR. MACPHAIL (*above the* R. *end of the table*). Not at all. It was only that your statement seemed to prove to me that every piece of good must be first contrasted to a piece of bad to make it a piece of good—but of course I'm only a doctor and these matters may be quite beyond my grasp.

REV. DAVIDSON (*sharply*). Precisely !

DR. MACPHAIL. What is beyond my grasp, is how you have the heart to send that poor thing back to three years in an American prison.

REV. DAVIDSON. Don't you see ? It's necessary ! Do you think my heart doesn't bleed for her. I love her as I love my wife and sister. All the time she is in prison I shall suffer all the pain she suffers !

DR. MACPHAIL. Bunkum ! (*He sits on the upper corner of the table.*)

REV. DAVIDSON. You don't understand because you don't want to ! She's sinned and she must suffer. I know what she'll endure. So does she ! Her remorse, for all her sins is beautiful. I am humble and afraid. I am not worthy to touch the hem of her garment.

DR. MACPHAIL (*drawing his pipe*). We agree at last.

(DAVIDSON, *first in a reverie, makes no response to this. In fact, it is as though he has not really heard* MACPHAIL. *After a second he smiles at* MACPHAIL *as one would at a foolish child, picks up his hat, rises, and starts toward the verandah.*)

MRS. DAVIDSON (*anxiously following* DAVIDSON). Alfred, you aren't going out, are you ?

REV. DAVIDSON (*taking her hand in his with one of his rare demonstrations of affection*). Go to bed, my wife. It is getting late. You look wan and pale.

MRS. DAVIDSON (*her voice changing almost to one of pleading*). Alfred, don't go out again tonight, please don't ; it's not healthy. It has rained for four days now and the air is full of poison from rotting plants. Besides, I want to talk to you. I—I—have not had a word alone with you, Alfred, for a long time.

REV. DAVIDSON. My poor wife. I know—I know—but I must ! I must.

(*He exits through the verandah.*)

MRS. DAVIDSON (*turning; unhappily*). He prayed with Miss Thompson last night until she went to sleep. It was nearly three o'clock when he came upstairs. Then, he threw himself down on the bed exhausted—but he only slept in snatches. He has strange dreams that puzzle him. (*Sitting in the deck-chair.*) He'll have a breakdown if he doesn't take care. This morning he told me he had been dreaming about the mountains of Nebraska.

DR. MACPHAIL (*reflectively*). H-m ! That's odd !

MRS. DAVIDSON. I don't believe anyone but myself realizes what an enormous amount of emotional force my husband puts into his work.

DR. MACPHAIL. Work is the one outlet for his tremendous energy that Mr. Davidson allows himself. He should look out.

MRS. DAVIDSON (*in a low voice*). The Lord's work is Mr. Davidson's life ! (*She pauses.*) On our wedding night Mr. Davidson explained to me his ideals of our marriage. He believed it should be a union free from earthly indulgence, devoted entirely to the salvation of others.

DR. MACPHAIL (*rising and moving to above the chair* R. *of* MRS. MACPHAIL). A noble doctrine, Mrs. Davidson, but to a medical man like myself, everyday experience proves that flesh and blood are not things apart from the spirit—each is mutually dependent upon the other—and their highest expression, strangely enough, is quite identical.

MRS. DAVIDSON (*sharply*). What do you mean ?

DR. MACPHAIL (*moving* R.C. *towards the verandah*). What I mean is this ! Natural emotions can never be denied—only disguised. (*He looks out across the verandah.*)

MRS. DAVIDSON. You are quite wrong. Both Mr. Davidson and I have high views on matters commonly accepted as part of human nature. I can safely say our marriage is entirely a contract of the spirit.

MRS. MACPHAIL (*anxious to smooth out a difficult moment*). And obviously a happy one. All marriages are happy where people have the same ambitions.

MRS. DAVIDSON (*becoming soft and human for the only time in the play*). Perhaps I had looked forward to a marriage of another sort. (*Her face grows wistful and sad.*) Like all women—I believe—I—wanted children. (*Long pause.*) But that was long ago. (*Her eyes are bright with tears.*) Sometimes I wonder a little. Two people as isolated and solitary as Mr. Davidson and myself . . . (*She pulls herself together.*) But no ! Mr. Davidson is right. (*She rises.*) There is only one course for those who work for others—

immolation of self—and sacrifice. (*She becomes her old, stiff, masked self.*) Goodnight.

(*She goes off upstairs quickly.*)

MRS. MACPHAIL (*a little awed*). I declare—I never realized that Mrs. Davidson was human.

DR. MACPHAIL (*turning*). It's highly probable she was born human. Most of us were !

MRS. MACPHAIL (*rolling up her sewing*). I think you are unfeeling, Robert, in your hard and fast diagnosis of others.

DR. MACPHAIL (*puffing his pipe as he moves to* C.). It is my business to diagnose, my dear. I am a doctor. (*He sits, thinking, in the chair* R. *of the table.*)

MRS. MACPHAIL (*rising and going over to him and yawning*). Well, you needn't work overtime on your friends.

DR. MACPHAIL (*patting her arm*). Everybody's conversation about everybody else is a diagnosis, my dear. In fact, you and I are now diagnosing each other—and my conclusion about you is ; to bed, to bed, you sleepy head. Shoo !

MRS. MACPHAIL (*kissing his bald spot*). Serious, silly old darling— Good night !

(*She exits upstairs.*)

(*A pause.* MACPHAIL *rises and crosses to the door of the store, opens it and looks in.*)

DR. MACPHAIL. Hello ! You still up, Horn ?

HORN (*answering*). Yep—reading. Want anything ?

DR. MACPHAIL. No—I'm off to bed.

(HORN *enters. His feet are bare. He wears frowzy pyjamas. He carries a bottle in one hand, a book in the other. He yawns and stretches. The two men listen to the rain.*)

Seems to be an uncanny concentation of malignancy about the rain tonight.

HORN (*crossing down and to* R.). H-m ! Perhaps. (*He goes to turn off the lamp.*) Everyone in ?

DR. MACPHAIL. Davidson's still out—can't sleep—has uneasy dreams his wife tells me. (*He goes as far as the stairs and starts to mount.*)

HORN. Can you see the landing ?

MACPHAIL. Yes. (*He stops.*) Eh, Horn, did you ever go through Nebraska on the train ?

HORN. Twenty years ago.

DR. MACPHAIL. Notice the mountains ?

HORN. Molehills, you mean.

DR. MACPHAIL. Call 'em what you like. They rose from the plain abruptly, remember—rounded, smooth. (*He starts toward stairs.*)

HORN (*turning the light very low*). Yep—what of it ?

DR. MACPHAIL. Didn't it strike you they were curiously like a woman's breasts ?

(MACPHAIL *exits upstairs.*)

(HORN *proceeds to turn out the lamp as he leisurely digests* MACPHAIL'S *last remark. A flicker of understanding crosses his face. He takes a long look at* SADIE'S *door, then gives a short laugh, as though to say " Well, well, well ! " He blows out the lamp and exits, leaving the stage in darkness. The stage is empty for a full minute. Through the increasing fury of the rain the plaintive whine of the reed instruments persists. Then the door of* SADIE'S *room opens and she totters out. She carries a little hand lamp. In the wan light of the lamp her face is ghastly with suffering. She makes her way to the staircase and calls up pitifully.*)

SADIE (*calling up the stairs*). Reverend Davidson ! Reverend Davidson !

(*There is no answer.* SADIE *crosses the stage to the hatrack, notes that* DAVIDSON'S *hat is gone. She sighs, seats herself on* HORN'S *deck-chair, her chin in her hands, staring at nothing.* DAVIDSON *enters from the verandah. He is like a man in a trance, his eyes glazed.* SADIE *gives a little cry and rises, seeing him as he crosses to* C. *He is hatless and rain soaked.*)

REV. DAVIDSON. Is that you, Miss Thompson ? (*Moving down* L. *of* SADIE.) What are you up for ?
SADIE. I couldn't sleep—this rain—and those drums—and then thinking about tomorrow. I couldn't seem to stand it in there another moment. I don't seem to be able to do much by myself, do I ?
REV. DAVIDSON. Not yet, maybe, but every prayer is going to make you stronger.
SADIE (*sinking into the chair again*). This time tomorrow I'll be on the sea—all by myself. I don't suppose I'll ever see you again.
REV. DAVIDSON. Not in this life, Sadie, probably.
SADIE. I'll be in prison three years. That's a long time. What'll I do when I come out ? What'll I be ? For hours and hours I've been wondering.
REV. DAVIDSON (*giving her a strange look*). Out there in the rain (*he points*) I walked and wondered too. The darkness was full of eyes. I saw things I never saw before. I looked into the awful groves of Ashtoreth where Solomon went—to find the secrets of joy and terror. I saw Ashtoreth herself—I saw Judas. Sadie, you don't have to go back to San Francisco.
SADIE (*giving him a blank stare*). I don't have to go back ? What do you mean ?
REV. DAVIDSON. I repeat—you do not have to go back . . . unless you truly want to.

SADIE. But I do want to. What sacrifice can I make to God but that ? I haven't got anything else to offer. It's the only thing that I've got to give. I want to give it—I must !

REV. DAVIDSON (*in a voice shaken with emotion*). Thank God ! Thank God !

SADIE. Why do you say that, Mr. Davidson ?

REV. DAVIDSON. Because you said what I knew you'd say. My every prayer has been answered. I prayed that there might come into your heart so passionate a desire for this punishment which you now lay as a thank-offering at your Redeemer's feet, that even if I offered to let you go, you would refuse.

SADIE (*faintly*). I hope I'll be strong enough to go through with it right !

REV. DAVIDSON. From now on you will be strong—there's to be no more fear. (*He now speaks as though in ecstasy.*) Beautiful, radiant, you will be one of the daughters of the King. (*He bends over her and speaks in a curiously hoarse whisper.*) That's what you are now, Sadie—one of the daughters of the King—radiant—beautiful.

SADIE (*tottering to her feet*). I'm going to see if I can't get some sleep. Good night !

(*She picks the lamp from the stool and exits slowly.*)

DAVIDSON *stands as though hypnotized, watching her. For a brief moment he seems to gain control of his emotions, then strides toward her door and stops abruptly outside it. Suddenly his head droops, his hands clasp convulsively, and a bitter struggle between* DAVIDSON, *the man of* GOD, *and* DAVIDSON, *human creature, takes place. His head and shoulders now square and with studied deliberation he grasps the handle of* SADIE'S *door, opens it, and steps inside, slowly closing the door after him. The rain is now almost a cloudburst and*

the CURTAIN *falls.*

SCENE 2

It is morning when the curtain lifts again. The night and the rain have passed. The place is flooded in sunshine. Immediately one is aware of hub-bub within and without.

At the verandah rail stand two natives. They are pointing and crying out. Some horrible object lying on the ground below is the cause of this commotion. Into the scene rushes a native POLICEMAN *from down* R. *He crosses the stage and enters* HORN'S *store. We hear his excited news and* HORN'S *exclamations of horror.*

HORN (*off stage*). Ki-Kai-Awana.
POLICEMAN (*off stage*). Fi-lo-kipi-manuva.
HORN (*off stage*). Mona-lava. Far-fali-oka.
POLICEMAN (*off stage*). Ki-kai-Awana.

(*The store door opens and* HORN *enters, followed by the* POLICEMAN.)

HORN. Oh ! Talofi-Talofi. Dreadful, dreadful ! (*He stumbles upstairs calling.*) Dr. MacPhail ! Dr. MacPhail !

(*Piercing cries are heard, and a* NATIVE GIRL *rushes in from the verandah.*)

NATIVE GIRL (*on the verandah step*). Jujuouija kepi lay manuva !

(*The girl's eyes are dilated with fear. There is chaotic clamouring from all the natives, who join her on the step. The* POLICEMAN *roughly pushes them out of the scene.*)

HORN (*at the top of the stairs*). Doctor ! Doctor !
DR. MACPHAIL (*upstairs, off stage*). Yes, yes ! What is it ?
HORN (*disappearing up the stairs*). Get up ! Right away !
DR. MACPHAIL. What is it ?
HORN (*off*). Hurry up ! Get up right away !
DR. MACPHAIL (*off stage*). All right, just a minute.
HORN (*re-appearing and coming down the stairs*). Hurry, doctor !
DR. MACPHAIL (*off stage*). All right ! All right ! I'll be right down !

(HORN *stumbles downstairs again. Following him comes* DR. MACPHAIL *in pyjamas and raincoat, his hair sleepily tousled. He carries a medicine kit which he has picked up in his rush.*)

HORN. Hurry—hurry—hurry !
DR. MACPHAIL. All right ! Here I am ! What is it ?
HORN. It's Davidson ! Something terrible has happened !

(HORN *rushes out to the verandah, followed by* MACPHAIL. HORN *stands looking out over the verandah. The* DOCTOR, *after a quick glance over the verandah rail, hurriedly exits down* R. HORN *shouts to the natives below.*)

78

Boys ! Don't touch that body until the Doctor gets there !
NATIVE VOICES (*off stage*). O-lan-sta-doctwr.

(*The door of the store opens and* MRS. HORN *waddles on. She starts to cross to the verandah but is intercepted by* SERGEANT O'HARA, *who comes tearing around the upstage verandah entrance at that moment. He is still dressed in his blue denim and is visibly excited.*)

O'HARA (*up* R.C., *to* MRS. HORN). Where's Miss Thompson ?
MRS. HORN. She sleep I think.
O'HARA. Sure ?
MRS. HORN. I make knock, what !?
O'HARA. No ! If she's asleep, let her sleep.

(*He crosses to the stairway and looks upstairs.* MRS. HORN *continues to the verandah.*)

MRS. HORN (*on the verandah; wringing her hands*). Mamut ! Mamut !
HORN (*calling from the verandah*). Doctor ! How long has he been dead ?
DR. MACPHAIL (*responding off stage*). Three or four hours, I should judge.
HORN (*turning back into the room and crossing to* R. *of the table*). I hope they don't bring him in here. I don't like men who die that way. They don't rest easy.

(MRS. HORN *exits down* R. *to the scene of the tragedy, snivelling as she goes*—HORN *turns and sees* O'HARA.)

Pretty rotten business this. How did you know about it ?
O'HARA (*coming down to above the table*). One of the mess boys— out fishing early—saw him and came for me. I got over here as fast as I could in case Sadie needed me. (*An apprehensive look comes over his face.*) You don't think (*brokenly*)—there isn't any chance Sadie did it ?
HORN (*waving his hand reassuringly*). No ! Some native fisherman saw him do it himself. They brought the body here.
O'HARA (*relieved*). Thank God ! How long has he been dead ?
HORN. Three or four hours MacPhail says. (*He becomes greatly agitated and mops his brow.*) I've got to get Mrs. Davidson.

(MRS. MACPHAIL *is heard coming downstairs.*)

O'HARA (*quickly*). Get her to do it !
MRS. MACPHAIL (*rushing into the room from the stairs. Her hair is frowsy and she is still hooking up her dress*). What has happened ? Where's Dr. MacPhail gone ? (*She comes down between* HORN *and* O'HARA.)
HORN. He's down on the beach, ma'am. (*Both men try to avoid her eyes.*)
MRS. MACPHAIL (*persistently*). What has happened ?
O'HARA (*evasively*). There's been an accident, ma'am.

MRS. MACPHAIL.   Is it Miss Thompson ?
O'HARA.   No !

(MRS. MACPHAIL *suddenly rushes for the verandah. Both men make a belated effort to follow and stop her. She reaches the verandah and leans over and looks down the beach.* O'HARA *and* HORN *stand watching her.*)

MRS. MACPHAIL.   What is that crowd doing ?

(*Suddenly she screams and rushes back into the room, her hands over her eyes.* HORN *puts out his hand and pulls her toward him, trying to calm her. She looks up at* HORN'S *face.*)

I was afraid of this !
HORN (*astonished*).   *You* were afraid ?

(HORN *and* MRS. MACPHAIL *are now* R.C.   O'HARA *is above and on their* R.)

MRS. MACPHAIL (*almost convulsively, as* HORN *takes her down to the deck-chair*).   Yes.   Mrs. Davidson heard you come up for Dr. MacPhail.   She's just been in my room and in a dreadful state. Mr. Davidson hasn't been to bed at all, she said.   She heard him leave Miss Thompson's room about three.   He came upstairs for something—then he went right out.

(DR. MACPHAIL *enters hurriedly from the verandah and crosses* L.C. *He places his medicine kit on the table.*

(*She rushes to* DR. MACPHAIL.)   Is he dead ?
DR. MACPHAIL (*in a quiet and professional tone*).   Yes !   Go and get Mrs. Davidson at once !
MRS. MACPHAIL (*tearfully*).   Oh, but I hate to !
DR. MACPHAIL (*curtly*).   You must, my dear !   (*As she hesitates.*) Be quick.

(MRS. MACPHAIL *goes upstairs in terrified obedience.* DR. MACPHAIL *turns to the two men.   He extends his clenched fist to* HORN, *as though indicating something in it.* HORN *moves up to him.*)

DR. MACPHAIL.   The razor was still in his hand.

(HORN *and* O'HARA *nod understandingly.*)

The Naval doctors are with him now.   They'll probably take him to the mortuary.

(MACPHAIL *walks to the foot of the stairs and stands waiting for* MRS. DAVIDSON.   HORN *and* O'HARA *give each other searching looks.*)

O'HARA (*looking over the verandah*).   Look at the crowd.   Bad news travels, don't it ?
HORN.   Yes.   (*Looks quizzically at* O'HARA.)   He was a strange fellow.   I wonder why he did it.

DR. MACPHAIL (*turning to* HORN *and* O'HARA). Be quiet ! Here comes Mrs. Davidson.

(*All three men stand by quietly as* MRS. DAVIDSON *enters down the stairway, followed by* MRS. MACPHAIL. *She is dressed in black, her face is blanched and drawn. She stands on the lower stairs, looking at* DR. MACPHAIL, *who is facing her.*)

MRS. DAVIDSON (*brokenly*). Where am I—to go ?
DR. MACPHAIL (*offering her his hand and speaking very kindly*). Come with me, Mrs. Davidson. (*He looks up at his wife.*) Better come too, Margaret. It may be necessary.

(*They start toward the verandah.* MRS. MACPHAIL *haltingly following* MRS. DAVIDSON *and* DR. MACPHAIL. HORN *and* O'HARA *watch them silently. As the trio exit,* O'HARA *turns to* HORN.)

O'HARA. Pretty cool, I'll say.
HORN (*shaking his head*). No—she's trembling like a leaf.
O'HARA (*as though to himself*). I wonder how she'll take it.
HORN. I wonder !

(*Suddenly the raucous sound of the gramophone is heard from* SADIE'S *room. Both men start, listen, and then turn to each other with a look of tempered horror.*)

My God ! Listen to that !
O'HARA. You see—she don't know yet.
HORN (*excitedly*). But—man—why is she playing it ?
O'HARA. One of us ought to go in and tell her what's happened.
HORN (*giving* O'HARA *a keen look*). She hasn't touched that thing since Davidson went after her. (*He takes a step toward* O'HARA *and looks intently into his face.*) What's she playing it now for ?
O'HARA (*shifting uneasily on his feet, his head down and speaking almost solemnly*). I don't know.
HORN (*trying to arrive at a conclusion and pointing his words*). Look-a-here ! Last night she was frightened and all-in about going back to San Francisco. (*He pauses and fires his question.*) Why is she playing that thing first thing this morning when at noon she's leaving on a journey she's scared to make ? (*He pauses and almost shouts.*) Why ?
O'HARA (*looking at him doggedly*). How should I know ?
HORN (*quizzically*). What do you infer ?
O'HARA (*roughly*). I am not inferring !
HORN. Who's going to tell her ? You ?
O'HARA. It'll come better from you.
HORN (*sighs resignedly*). All right ! Go see where the others are.

(HORN *shuffles up to* SADIE'S *door.* O'HARA *waits an instant as though undecided as to what to do, then thrusting his chin up determindedly he crosses to the verandah and exits.*)

Miss Thompson ! (*He knocks on the door.*)

SADIE (*from within her room*). Yes ! (*Loudly.*) What is it ?

HORN. Let me in. It's Horn !

SADIE (*from within the room*). Oh, no you don't ! You stay where you are ! I'll be out in a minute.

HORN (*above* SADIE'S *doorway*). It's most important, Miss Thompson.

SADIE (*from within her room*). All right ! I'm coming right out !

(HORN *shuffles to a position in front of the sofa as* SADIE'S *door opens and* SADIE *makes her appearance. She is dressed in the costume in which we first beheld her. Her face is tragic beneath its rouge. She carries her parasol. As she enters the room* O'HARA *comes across the verandah and, upon seeing* SADIE, *he halts at* R.C., *as though stupefied.*)

(*To* HORN.) Hello, Horn ! What's going on ? (*She turns and sees* O'HARA. *With a forced smile.*) Hello, O'Hara ! What are you doing up so early ? (*She crosses* HORN *to* L. *of the table.*)

O'HARA (*looking dazedly at* SADIE). Sadie !

SADIE (*smiling, but one corner of her mouth seems rather down*). Surprised to see me all dolled up, eh ? Well, why not ? (*She is making a desperate attempt to be cheerful.*) Had to put on my best, didn't I ? This gay and glorious morning. Besides (*her face hardens*) I'm radiant—I'm beautiful. You didn't know that, did you ? (*She laughs harshly.*) Couldn't believe my eyes when I saw that sun this morning. Do I feel fine ? I do ! I'd race you down to the beach if it wasn't for these pesty heels. (*She flicks her heels to the tip of her parasol, moving to above and* L. *of the table.*)

O'HARA (*moving to above the table*). Sadie ! For God's sake turn off that gramophone !

SADIE (*coolly*). And why—for God's sake should I turn off the gramophone ?

O'HARA. They'll be back any minute.

SADIE. Who ?

O'HARA. Mrs. Davidson.

SADIE (*assuming an attitude of studied indifference*). And why should I turn off my gramophone because Mrs. Davidson is coming back ? (*An almost snarling sneer comes into her voice.*) I am not concerned with what Mrs. Davidson thinks, and for that matter (*she turns and looks at* HORN) with what your Reverend Davidson thinks ! (*She faces downstage and speaks deliberately.*) My advice to him is to pin on his wings and try the air !

O'HARA (*suddenly to* HORN). Joe, turn off that gramophone, quick !

(HORN *starts to* SADIE'S *door.*)

SADIE (*turning quickly to* HORN *as he reaches the door*). Stay out of my room, Horn ! That gramophone stays on.

O'HARA (*pleading*). Sadie ! Something has happened !

SADIE (*in a voice black with loathing*).   Yes !—You're right !
Something *has* happened. You men ! Something *has* happened !
(*To* HORN.) You men—you're all alike. (*Hoarsely*.) Pigs ! Pigs !
I wouldn't trust one of you ! (*She turns quickly toward* O'HARA.)
No offence to you in that last remark, old pardner. (*She pauses*.)
And I'm going to Sydney if that invitation of yours still holds good.
    O'HARA (*his voice broken with emotion*).   You bet it does !

(HORN *motions to* O'HARA *to tell* SADIE *what has happened*. O'HARA
                          continues.)

Sadie—Davidson's killed himself—
    SADIE (*dully*). What ?
    O'HARA.   They found him on the beach this morning in the
water with his throat cut.

(*As the import of what* O'HARA *has said penetrates* SADIE'S *whirling
    brain, she staggers, then slowly recovers herself*.)

    SADIE (*in a strange voice, moving down below the table to* R.C.).
So—he killed himself, did he ? Then I can forgive him. I thought
the joke was on me—all on me ! (*Pauses*.) I see it wasn't.

(O'HARA *moves to above the* R. *end of the table*. DR. MACPHAIL
            rushes in, gesticulating angrily.)

    DR. MACPHAIL (*on the verandah step*).   What the devil are you
doing ? Stop that damn machine ! Mrs. Davidson's coming !
    SADIE (*weakly, turning up* R.C.). Yes—turn it off—off.

(HORN *rushes into* SADIE'S *room and stops the gramophone*.)

(MRS. DAVIDSON *enters, followed by* MRS. MACPHAIL. MRS.
    DAVIDSON *walks straight toward* SADIE, *crossing below the table*.
    *There is intense silence on the stage. The two women gaze intently
    at each other*.)

    MRS. DAVIDSON (*sadly*). I understand, Miss Thompson. I'm
sorry for him and I'm sorry for you.

(MRS. DAVIDSON *passes her, hastily, covers her face and walks
                          upstairs*.)

(*All the people on the stage watch her until she is out of sight*.)

    SADIE (*in a low, sick voice*). I'm sorry for everybody in the world!
Life's a quaint present from somebody, there's no doubt about that.
(*Moving to* O'HARA.) Maybe it will be easier in Sydney.

     She clutches O'HARA'S *arm and breaks into sobs as*

                   the CURTAIN *falls*.

FURNITURE AND PROPERTY PLOT

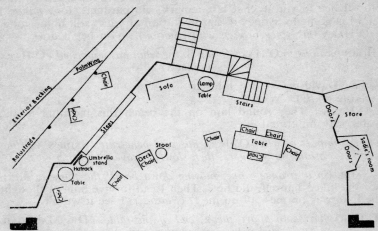

Cloth on stage. Various strips of old matting.
Shabby carpet on stairs.
On the walls:—
   Lithograph of Queen Alexandra (*above oak lamp table*).
   Lithograph of President Garfield (L. *of stairs*).
   Old map of American Samoa (*underneath the above*).
   (*The above are suggestions only of the type of pictures required. Ohters may be added or substituted.*)
   Miniature ship in two-gallon bottle, at L. wall.
   Stuffed seagull above SADIE'S doorway.
   Old Japanese bead curtain over SADIE'S doorway.
Bamboo rain shutters for the verandah—practical.
One shabby sofa (*preferably in maroon plush*).
Carved oak table (*round or octagonal*).
   On it:—Lamp and shade as described.
Hat rack. Receptacle—tall pot or barrel—with old umbrella.
Two rattan upright chairs (*at* R.) in room.
Two ditto, on the verandah (*or iron café chairs*).
One small café table, R.
One rattan deck-chair (*at* R.C.)
One stool or coffee table (L. *of deck-chair*).
   On it:—Box of cigars. Battered volume of Nietzche.
One small dining table, covered with old red cloth.
   On it:—Salt cellars, castors, sugar bowls.
      (*All the above covered over with pieces of mosquito netting.*)
Five iron café chairs at the table. (*These to be painted green.*)

PROPS.—ACT I.

Ready off R. (*for the natives at opening of Act*):—
>   Basket of pineapples.
>   Basket of sundry fruit.
>   Basket of native toys and masks.
>   Pole with fish bladders and pieces of dried shark.
>   Basket of flowers to braid wreaths.

PERSONAL.
>   HORN.   Cigarettes, matches, half-pint bottle of whisky.
>   MRS. HORN.   Feather duster.
>   MRS. DAVIDSON.   Pince-nez.
>   NATIVES (*later entrance*).   Boxes of tobacco, etc.
>   SADIE.   Several bundles tied in shawls, etc.   Battered suitcase.   Portable gramophone.   Two or three dance records.   Lingerie and sundry clothes and belongings.   Small bottle of whisky.   Packet of cigarettes.   Matches.

PROPS.—ACT II.

>   Lamp from oak table, ready in store off L. for MRS. HORN.
>   Dinner bell ready off L. for native girl.
>   Tin of tomales and small pitcher of water, ready in store for SADIE.
>   Trays with dishes, cutlery, and food, ready L. in store for MRS. HORN.

PERSONAL.
>   HORN.   Piece of mosquito netting over face.   Whisky bottle.
>   DR. MACPHAIL.   Pipe, tobacco, matches, as before.
>   SADIE.   Cigarettes, matches, banana or apple.
>   MRS. DAVIDSON.   Needlework bag, containing work.
>   MRS. MACPHAIL.   Ditto.
>   O'HARA.   Cigarettes and matches.
>   NATIVE.   Letter in an envelope.

PROPS.—ACT III, *Scene* 1.

>   Ready off L. in SADIE'S room :—
>   SADIE'S luggage, packed, with long loose coat.

PERSONAL.
>   SADIE.   Old dressing gown (*white towelling*) hand lamp or candle.
>   GRIGGS.   Small basket of pineapples or other fruit.
>   MRS. HORN.   Palm leaf fan.
>   HORN.   Book.

PROPS.—ACT III, *Scene* 2.

PERSONAL.
>   DR. MACPHAIL.   Medical kit bag.   (*This to contain an old razor for later entrance.*)

LIGHTING PLOT

ACT I.

To open:—

FLOATS.   Amber, pink and blue, full.

No. 1 BATTEN.   Amber, pink, blue and white, full.

OTHER BATTENS.   Amber, pink and blue, full.

FLOOD *on exterior*.   White and straw.

STAGE FLOOD (*through verandah*).   No. 51 gold and white frost.

INTERIOR BACKINGS.   Amber lengths.

CUE.   *As* SADIE *exits with marines*.   Commence slow check of all lighting to half, except whites which fade to NIL.   Change flood on exterior slowly to No. 16 steel frost, well checked down, mingled with a little deep amber.

NOTE.—*Stage lighting may be brought up and down during the Act, subsequently, as desired for effect.*)

ACT II

To open:—

FLOATS.   Amber, pink and blue, at quarter.

No. 1 BATTEN.   Amber, pink and blue, threequarters.

OTHER BATTENS.   Ditto, at half.

(*The above to be checked slightly as the Act proceeds.*)

FLOOD *on exterior*.   Mingled amber and salmon pink.

(*Amber in above to change to No. 18 blue later, as directed.*)

STAGE FLOOD.   No. 4 amber, at half (*to fade later*).

CUE.   Bring in gold pool of light around small table up R., as MRS. HORN lights table lamp.

ACT III

Scene 1.

FLOATS.   Amber and blue only, at quarter.

No. 1 BATTEN.   Amber and blue only, at half.

OTHER BATTENS.   Blue only at quarter.

HANGING LAMP.   ON.   No. 51 gold spot on C. acting area.
(*Check spot to half and all ambers OUT as* HORN *turns down the lamp. Further check of spot as he turns lamp down still lower.*)

FLOOD *on Exterior*.   No. 20 blue, at half.

Scene 2.

Lighting as for the opening of Act I.

No CUES.

Any character costumes or wigs needed in the performance of this play can be hired from Charles H. Fox Ltd, 25 Shelton Street, London WC2

MADE AND PRINTED IN GREAT BRITAIN BY
BUTLER & TANNER LTD, FROME AND LONDON
MADE IN ENGLAND